MW00849559

Shifting into Purer Consciousness

Integrating Spiritual Transformation with the Human Experience

YVONNE PERRY

Write On! Publishing
Nashville, Tennessee

What People Are Saying about *Shifting into Purer Consciousness*

SHIFTING INTO PURER CONSCIOUSNESS is a marvelous book filled with so much valuable information. Yvonne Perry provides just about everything you need to know to support your journey through the ascension process, which is a path from chaos to peace.

The book is obviously based on Ms. Perry's careful research, hard life lessons, and her innate intuitive skills. Ms. Perry's writing has an inner clarity that makes difficult subjects easy to understand. The timely arrival of this book will provide so much help for so many people.

~ Hannah Beaconsfield, author of *Welcome to Planet Earth: A Guide for Walk-ins, Starseeds, and Lightworkers*

~~~~~~~~~~

We've heard so much about the coming shift in our world, but Yvonne Perry's *Shifting into Purer Consciousness* is the first truly practical manual for navigating the ascension process. This enables anyone who wishes to raise one's frequency to have a perfect pathway for ascendency and become the pure light of grace on the planet.

~ Jackie Lapin, author of the award-wining bestseller *Practical Conscious Creation: Daily Techniques to Manifest Your Desires* (www.jackielapin.com)

~~~~~~~~~~

In this time of material and political upheaval, many people are experiencing a rapid, positive, spiritual shift in consciousness and even biology. Yvonne Perry's new book is a fascinating look at what this all means and how to be a conscious participant.

~ Andrew Cort, author of *Symbols, Meaning, and the Sacred Quest: Spiritual Awakening in Jewish, Christian, and Islamic Stories*

Yvonne Perry shares her stories, symptoms, and tips of her journey on the path of spiritual awakening. *Shifting into Purer Consciousness* gives you tools for an easier integration of your Soul, Christ Self, and Divine God Self into your physical body. This book can make your shift of consciousness easier.

~ Michael David Lawrience, energy healer and author of *The Secret for Freedom from Drama, Trauma, and Pain*

~~~~~~~~~~

Yvonne Perry has a way of energetically infusing the reader with information that resonates so deeply, you are transformed immediately. *SHIFTING INTO PURER CONSCIOUSNESS* opens the way to embrace the vibrational shift of the planet with grace and ease while giving reason to the unreasonable. The answers you have been searching for are now here.

~ Harriette Knight, master healer, author, and radio host

~~~~~~~~~~

Yvonne Perry is gifted with the spiritual savvy and skills to discuss complex issues such as ascension, walk-in/out experiences, near-death or out-of-body experiences, downloading from higher dimensions, and merging with over souls to help people utilize multifaceted information helpful to shift into a higher state. Through integrating new energy—life-sustaining frequencies of the universe, we are now able to transcend the limits of our physical challenges to embrace our divine multidimensional selves. This higher state of being is happening to those willing to embrace the oneness and interconnected energetic universal life force.

Ms. Perry's new book, *Shifting into Purer Consciousness*, helps to demystify ancient mystical concepts and to apply practical ways to support the present day human and spiritual experience of transformation. Through illuminating the journey of the soul at this time of immense change, healing for the planet and our human condition is the possible and hoped for outcome. At this time of great transformation, personal and collective structures and belief systems that no longer support the highest good of humanity will be shed in order to bring in a more valued understanding of the oneness and sacredness of life.

~ Sheryl Iris Glick, Reiki master teacher, author of *Life is No Coincidence*, and host of the Internet radio show, Healing from Within

~~~~~~~~~~

Yvonne's book, *Shifting into Pure Consciousness,* was a real page-turner for me! It was so reassuring that we each have choices to our thoughts, and that our thoughts really can shape our lives... for the better. Not only while here on planet earth, but as we ascend into even greater realms.

Over the past few years I've come to a place of not fearing death, but instead embracing the beauty of what this means for the next steps on my journey. Yvonne's book has helped me take that up another notch with understanding that if we are open to all the possibilities, it will positively enhance where we are *right now in this moment*. And the most comforting thing is knowing we truly are, as Yvonne says, "You and me—everyone on the planet—standing side by side in unity and oneness. We really are one." And most powerful and deeply touching for me is realizing that this means whether we are here in physical body or not, that we are, and will always be, connected.

~ Barbara Techel, award-winning author, www.joyfulpaws.com

~~~~~~~~~~

It was with much delight and gratitude that I was reading Yvonne's new book. It really explains what is going on in the universe, our planet, and with ourselves. The provided information and tools will be very helpful for all readers to heal the mindset of separation and transform unresolved personal issues and emotions. It is important to understand the ascension process, which comes after resurrection, but there is no resurrection until something—the EGO—dies. The author understands that the process might be scary at times, but is a guide through this challenging time. We are following Jesus and other spiritual masters if we embrace that this process is an opportunity of great spiritual growth.

Thanks for explaining the walk-in of LavendarRose; all readers will benefit from her teachings and I highly recommend that you honor this information by working with all the valuable prayers, exercises, affirmations, links, quotes, and the wonderful vibration of this masterpiece.

~ Eva-Maria Mora, author of *Quantum Angel Healing: Energy Therapy and Communication with Angels*

~~~~~~~~~

Shifting into Purer Consciousness is astonishing in its breadth and depth of knowledge in what it means to be a spirit being in human form at this particular time. Never will we find as truthful and candid a discussion of the human condition and ascension consciousness. One must admire the freedom with which the myriad of spiritual experiences and paths to a purer consciousness are described, and accessible. Undoubtedly, we are living in a decidedly crucial time in world and cosmic history. Moreover, each of us needs all the well-informed guidance available to become more fully human. Within these pages, we discover that vital guidance to help us in finding our way. For religions fail us, but God provides our spiritual food in grace and in abundance.

~ S. L. (Steve) Brannon, interfaith spiritual minister and author of *The Two Agreements: A Good News Story for Our Time*

Award-winning author Yvonne Perry provides a thorough, well-researched resource for those spiritually-awakening people who are also questioning or are confused about the events in their lives. Perry likens the spiritual awakening to an ascension through which people integrate refined or "purer" energies. Each person experiencing this process will find phenomenal resources and explanations for managing their spiritual integration in this book. Do you need to refine your personal judgments? Are you experiencing the ups and downs of an emotional roller coaster? Do you need support for physical problems? Do you need to know why the events are happening right now? Perry explains with uncanny thoroughness the answers to why and how each one of us might experience our personal version of the planetary and cosmic shifts. I've always admired Perry's ability to explain spiritual events on a personal level and bring it home for the reader. *Shifting into Purer Consciousness* is one of her best yet.

~ Dr. Caron Goode, author of From *Fizzle to Sizzle: 4 Crucial Tools for Relationship Repair,* and founder of the Academy for Coaching Parents International

Contents

Acknowledgments

To my parents, who, along with my grandmother, raised me to honor and love Jesus Christ. Many thanks to Bon, who brought this body into incarnation and allowed me to step in when she completed her mission.

Love and thanks to Randy, who inspires me to keep moving forward on my spiritual path.

To Caron and Ranoli, who encouraged me to write this book.

Heartfelt thanks to Vickie Majors, who created the beautiful artwork for the book's cover, and to graphic designer, Rick Chappell, for the layout.

A special thanks to Dr. Susan Allison for writing the foreword.

Appreciation goes to Rick Lewis, who formatted the bibliography, and to Dana Micheli, who edited the manuscript. Cheers to all those who helped with proofreading!

Thank you to the Holy Spirit, who comforts me and leads me into all truth.

To the Divine Mother, who nourishes me and gives grace, peace, and direction.

Gratitude to Mother Earth, who produces all resources that sustain my physical life.

Thanks to my guides and spirit companions who walk with me and keep my soul encouraged on the path to ascension.

My deep appreciation to the ascended masters who are helping humanity make the shift into purer consciousness.

Dedication

I dedicate this book to my grandchildren, who carry the light with an innate desire to participate in the process of spiritual transformation.

To the empaths, who read my book, *Whose Stuff Is This? Finding Freedom from the Thoughts, Feelings, and Energy of Those Around You*, and wrote such encouraging reviews, letting me know how much they appreciated having that tool for spiritual growth.

And, to all souls who are allowing the ascension to take place in their lives.

Other Books by Yvonne Perry

Whose Stuff Is This? Finding Freedom from the Thoughts, Feelings, and Energy of Those Around You is a resource for empathic people who have been unknowingly carrying energetic burdens that belong to someone else. Tips for using your intuitive ability as a tool for guidance without paying a personal price. http://Whosestuffisthis.com

More Than Meets the Eye: True Stories about Death, Dying, and Afterlife gives information about euthanasia, suicide, near-death experience, hospice care, assisting a dying loved one, spirit visits from deceased loved ones, and other topics that people are somewhat reluctant to talk about. Non-religious information and insight to assist people in finding peace about the mysterious process of transitioning back to God/Source. http://deathdyingafterlife.com

The Sid Series ~ A Collection of Holistic Stories for Children presents twelve stories focused on being true to one's self, overcoming fear, following inner guidance, caring for the body, dealing with change, coping with pet death, and seeing ghosts. http://TheSidSeries.com

Foreword

We live in an unprecedented time, a time of great change that some call "upheaval" or "chaos," and even "the time of the end." In a sense it is the end, but the end of a 5,125-year cycle of the Mayan calendar and the beginning of a new era for humankind, not a cataclysmic destruction of our planet. We are birthing a new world, and just like the birth process, it is also painful, messy, and work! However, birth is also uplifting, joy filled, and life changing. This more positive outlook, seeing 2012 as the birth of heaven on earth—a time of harmony and higher consciousness—depends on all of us, working individually and collectively, in order to bring it to fruition.

If we can see our embodiment at this time in history as our "choice," it then follows that we want to take responsibility for our part in the transformation of the planet. It is my belief that we each signed a contract between lives agreeing to come back at precisely this time to help usher in a new age of enlightenment and peace. Now it is our responsibility to raise our consciousness and vibration in order to come into alignment with our higher selves and fulfill our soul's purpose. How do we do this?

A good start is just what you're doing, reading Yvonne Perry's newest work, *Shifting into Purer Consciousness ~ Integrating Spiritual Transformation with the Human Experience*. Here, the author and metaphysical practitioner clearly explains what is happening on the planet and how each of us can navigate the rapid pace and accomplish our mission. Yvonne's approach is clear and organized, beginning with an overview of the energy shift on the planet from a scientific perspective, then offering a synopsis of the many prophecies about 2012, and progressively presenting chapters that help readers assess and understand where they are, who they are, and how to be the highest of "spiritual beings having a human existence."

Yvonne and I are so parallel in our lives at this time, and have been for many years, that it makes me laugh. Even my bumper sticker says, "We are spiritual beings having a physical experience!" We have never met in person, but she is my soul sister and in my soul family.

Actually, I first "met" Yvonne Perry by being a guest on her radio show, *We Are One in Spirit Podcast*, and then inviting her to be on my show, "Empowered Healer" on the Voice America, 7th Wave Network. From our first emails, and then definitely when conversing, I recognized Yvonne as a member of my soul family. I feel deeply connected to her, and as if I have known her for many years. This recognition is happening to many of us; everyone in our soul family is showing up now so we can join together as a team of lightworkers dedicated to changing ourselves, helping others come into alignment with their highest selves, and helping our planet shift.

Not only are we not alone on this spiritual path of ascension, with many people here joining with us, but Yvonne makes it clear that we are not alone in other ways. We have spiritual allies, ascended masters, and guides to call on any time, and they are waiting for us to do so. As Doreen Virtue says in her books, we all have guides and helpers, from spirit animal guides to angels ready and willing to be of assistance, but we need to ask first. Yvonne talks about connecting with our spirit allies through meditation, prayer, visualization, affirmation, chanting, and other means, using clear examples of these methods of connecting with our highest selves and the highest in the universe.

I encourage you to try some of the transformation tools that Yvonne offers. I know in my life that years of meditation, prayer, shamanic journey, the use of affirmations and journaling have been invaluable, and new and beautiful wisdom keeps coming in from former and current spirit helpers. Just a few days ago, while meditating, the archangel Metatron came in, and since then I can hear his voice helping me throughout each day. I feel grateful for this gift and can use all the help available!

When speaking of spirituality in this text, Yvonne is very respectful of every reader's belief system, and wants each of us to use whatever works for us as we connect with our inner spirit and with the creative force: God, Spirit, Source, Energy, Love, whatever we call this higher being. I love how Yvonne offers so many options and methods to help readers find what works for them. I also appreciate all of her personal stories about her religious background and her spiritual transformation, especially the discussion of her walk-in experience.

In her "walk-in," Yvonne describes her soul exchange, and the challenges and adjustments as well as the dividends of having a new soul with a higher frequency. When I read about her walk-in, I wondered if this could have been what happened to me. In 1994, just about everything in my life changed; I left a long-term marriage, became ill, met the love of my life, (who is now my husband), had many losses, moved several times, changed professions, and so on. What I remember is saying aloud to a creative writing class, "I need a huge change." Someone in the class reminded me a year or so later that I said this, but I had forgotten! What I do remember is that my soul felt like it was dying in the marriage, and not just in the marriage, but in my life in general. I did need a change and I got a big one that catapulted me into an entirely new and higher consciousness. Whether or not I am a "walk-in," Yvonne's chapter about her soul exchange has helped me understand my own evolution, and my guess is it will help you as well.

During 1994-1995 I remember telling my therapist that I thought I was having a nervous breakdown, that my heart was breaking, and she wisely said, "No, your heart is breaking open." I was having a spiritual awakening, and as Yvonne says, I was in the ascension process, and it hasn't let up since 1994. I love how Yvonne explains ascension several places in the text, as spiritual awakening, oneness, and conscious evolution, and then gives practical steps for handling any symptoms.

This explanation of symptoms and how to remedy them is my favorite part of the book because it is so practical and immediately helpful. Like Yvonne, I have or have had over 90 percent of the symptoms she lists, and I must say I feel relieved that I'm not falling apart, just in the process of rapid ascension! Some of the symptoms of spiritual awakening and transformation she lists are: hot and cold flashes, aches and pains, including headaches, anxiety and panic attacks, heart palpitations, synchronicities, and so on. From the discussion in the text, I now understand the connection to rapid evolution at a soul level, and what I've experienced makes more sense.

Another concept that resonates is about some of us being starseeds and lightworkers. Many of my clients, co-workers, and friends have talked about feeling like aliens here, as if they are from another galaxy, and I've felt this way, too. More than this, I truly have felt connected to the Pleiades and know on a deep intuitive level that I've been there or lived there. In the text, Yvonne speaks of starseeds being those who have been to other planets or stars, perhaps on their journey here or between lives on Earth, and this feels true for me. I've even studied with Barbara Hand-Clow and loved her book *The Pleiadian Agenda*. I've studied Barbara Marciniak's writings as well, and nearly underlined her entire book *Bringers of the Dawn* about Pleiadian wisdom. It felt and still feels like my own culture.

Also, I believe that many of us are lightworkers here to help the planet through the birth pangs and into a new age of harmony and unity. Most of the women in my groups want to shed what no longer serves them and focus intently on their mission here. As beings of light, we are to bring information to the planet that comes from our sacred heart space. Yvonne beautifully writes about the physical, spiritual, and sacred heart, and how we are to connect with our sacred heart and live from the higher truths therein.

It's interesting that many teachers (such as Drunvalo Melchizedek) are speaking of the sacred heart, and how to journey inside to meet the higher self and the God within us, to raise our vibration, to re-activate our DNA, and both draw in energy from the Light in the upper realms and send this healing light energy into the earth. In a sense, we are conduits or vessels that mediate between heaven and earth and help balance the energy of all there is. Before even hearing of Drunvalo, I've been leading meditations into the sacred heart space, and participants are meeting their higher selves and accessing wisdom to further their acceleration. Yvonne clearly shares the importance of this heart-based approach for all of us to use.

As stewards of the earth, each of us has a certain part to play, and this differs from person to person. *Shifting into Purer Consciousness* gives us the understanding and tools to navigate this intense time of rapid change, to BE the change by living our truth authentically and passionately. Yvonne Perry lights the way.

Susan Allison, Ph.D.

Santa Cruz, CA

April 13, 2012

INTRODUCTION

When I awoke at 3:38 a.m. on September 21, 2010, my mind was buzzing with thoughts about the tri-part aspect of our human experience as incarnated souls. I had been reading about soul, body, and perispirit in Allan Kardec's *The Spirits' Book* the day before. I tried to go back to sleep, but I started receiving inspiration that got my mental wheels turning. I laid there pondering for a while, but since I was wide awake I decided to get out of bed and write down my thoughts. As soon as my feet hit the floor I felt impressed to read the "Explanatory Notes" at the front of Kardec's book. I had skimmed over most of that section when I started the book.

After reading Kardec's Notes, I went to my computer to type some notes of my own about what I had just read. As I was putting that piece together for what I thought would be an article or a post for my blog, I began sensing an urge to write about my spiritually-transforming experiences—particularly the walk-in event that occurred in 1999. I had started working on that story many years ago, but had put it aside for a later date, sensing that there was more that I would add to it someday. I was right; even as I release this book, I remain a work in process and I'm sure there will be many more shifts in my consciousness and how I view spiritual concepts during this era called the Great Shift or Ascension.

Not sure how my walk-in related to the material I had read in *The Spirits' Book*, I opened the Word document that contained my notes from early 2005 and started reading. The strangeness I had felt as a soul still adjusting to being in a body had waned over the years; so, I was surprised by the feelings I had expressed when I first wrote about the walk-in. I sensed that my story would help souls who have recently walked in, and I needed to share it before I completely forgot what those early days were like.

As I added my thoughts and mentioned things that had happened since 2005, the document grew and grew—and so did my research. To say the least, the article or blog post I thought I was writing was too large to post online and I realized I was writing a book. I started to protest (something I've found totally useless when being led by Spirit to do something) because I was already in the process of writing *Whose Stuff Is This? ~ Finding Freedom from the Thoughts, Feelings, and Energy of Those around You,* which I published in February 2011. That book shares how I experienced hardship, fatigue, and total burnout as an untrained empath and what I did to overcome it. People who have read my empath book realize their responsibility for properly managing energy; and, they know how to protect their auric fields from psychic assault and what to do when they pick up detrimental energy for transmutation purposes. Though very difficult, my years as an untrained empath facilitated a soul shift or soul exchange (also known as a walk-in) and set the stage for me to begin the next phase of the ascension process, which I write about in the book you are now holding. At first, this book was going to be the full account of my walk-in experience. Then, I was urged to expand the scope and write about the accelerated cosmic frequencies now available to support our ascension process.

To support my findings, I read more than twenty books on the topic of spiritual development and the coming age of enlightenment— that's in addition to all the online research I conducted. Since I am well "versed" (pun intended) in the

> What we need is a book that supports the human experience of spiritual transformation.
>
> ~ Randall Hawk

Bible after spending forty years attending church three to five times per week, memorizing scripture, participating in prayer meetings, and playing keyboards as a member of the worship team, I use

Bible verses to support what I am relating in this book. I am not familiar with a lot of Eastern teachings and I wanted to get this book out within one year; so, a crash course in those ancient teachings was not an option. While this book can benefit anyone in any culture, it is intended to help those who are fearful of the future due to having been indoctrinated by fear-based religions that teach a dreadful end of time. So many of these dear ones are having experiences that do not align with their religion dogma and they are searching for answers.

Energies

Whenever we have a spiritually-transforming experience, we are left to wonder how to incorporate the new energies. If you've been led to this book, you have probably had or are experiencing some type of dramatic shift that has totally changed, or is changing your life. You may feel like a different person—and perhaps you are!

Soul

Your soul is ever expanding and you are integrating into your physical body the accelerated frequencies that came with that significant event. So, whether you had a walk-in/walk-out experience, a near-death or out-of-body episode, a download from a higher dimension, or a merging with your oversoul, *Shifting into Purer Consciousness* can help you make sense of what happened and give you tools to assist with integrating the new frequencies of your multidimensional self.

This book has exercises, affirmations, and visualizations to help anchor your light body and Christ oversoul as you raise the vibration of your physical body. The book is intended to help you move forward in your soul's personal evolution while helping others and the planet ascend into purer consciousness. While reading this material, you may sense an activation or clarification of your true purpose. You may discover why you are on the planet during such a time of transition.

Chapter 1 ~ Why All the Changes on Earth?

Everywhere I read these days someone is mentioning how our world seems to be going crazy. Many people are in crisis, strapped with fear, and stressed to the limit. People have lost jobs and financial security; there's an upheaval in government systems worldwide; the global economy could topple in a heartbeat; the religious institutions we once looked to for guidance are wrought with deceit; our youth are rioting; depression is rampant; health issues are escalating; and relationships are failing.

The negativity around us is so strong that some empathic people find it hard to even be in public. People who have always been emotionally strong are suddenly having panic and anxiety attacks. Those who have never considered themselves a "spiritual person" are praying, meditating, and seeking solace. Some say their dreams seem more real than the reality they have during waking hours.

What is going on here?

Everything is being shaken from within. It may feel or look bad during the process, but these systems and our old way of thinking are breaking down in order for us to create something new. A lot of

> The root cause of all suffering is the sense of separate existence.
>
> ~ Amma Bhagavan

what we are experiencing is our unresolved personal issues and cellular memory being pushed up and out as the "separation mindset" comes to the surface to be healed. On a collective level, there are seven primary karmic patterns that are being cleared and transcended at this time: arrogance, addiction, prejudice, hatred, shame, violence, and victimhood. These patterns are being exaggerated in order to bring them to our awareness so we can transform them.

Letting go of stuff that doesn't serve the Light can be scary. Families and relationships can be severely tested through financial hardship. Failing health hurts not only the body but also the mind and emotions. The process can get pretty messy and upsetting, but the end result will be a good thing and worth the effort it takes. Tested by fire, our souls will be refined as pure gold; the separate, fear-based mindset, controlled by the ego, will be overcome as we embrace the truth of our oneness with the Divine, our fellow humans, animals, and the Earth. In this book, I will give exercises to help you make this process as gentle, easy, and fast as possible.

Earth Expansion

The Earth—Mother Gaia—is a living being. She has consciousness and emits Her own frequencies to the universe and Her inhabitants. She has Her own troubles right now; She is going through a major cleansing as She loses magnetism and her vibration is rising in frequency. For as long as scientists have been measuring the Earth's pulse or vibration, it remained consistent at 7.8 cycles per second until 1987, when it began increasing. This is when we entered the final transition period on the Mayan calendar. By 1996, it had increased to about 9 cycles per second. It is predicted that by December 2012 the Earth's pulse will be at about 13 cycles per second. As a result of this vibrational increase, tsunamis, earthquakes, floods, hurricanes, global warming, and volcanic activity have devastated certain areas on our planet. In 2010, US natural disasters doubled that of any single year since 1999.

The physical changes we are witnessing are also due to the accelerated energy around our planet. Solar flares, comets, and meteorites are plenteous. According to scientists, the Earth is entering alignment with the equator of the Milky Way Galaxy as it does every 12,000 or so Earth years. The Earth has gone through several biological ascensions in Her history and is going through yet another expansion process. We are interconnected with the planet and everything on it and thus, as the planet is evolving, we are feeling this urge to purge—inward and outward. When we pay attention and ask for guidance, we will be able to discern what these upsetting events signify and know that there is a spiritual purpose to all the changes we see going on around us.

This faster vibration is expanding the electromagnetic field that surrounds the Earth. Anyone who is sensitive to energy is feeling this expansion and increase in vibration. This shift is affecting a lot of people emotionally because it is transcending long-held thought patterns and integrating new patterns necessary to ascend into a purer consciousness and less dense matter.

I expect to see continued changes in the way we communicate; we are becoming more telepathic. The recent generation of children is psychically aware unlike any we have ever seen. They are helping to usher in the new paradigm.

How Human Energy Affects the Earth

Earth's increase in frequency is obviously affecting us, and in return our attitudes, beliefs, actions, and collective vibration are affecting the Earth. We used to think that matter was solid and that we were all divided individuals, but now we are aware that an atom is comprised of almost entirely empty space. Scientifically, we are all part of a matrix or field of energy. Our current reality is a picture of where our energy is or has been focused individually and collectively. We are in a time of great transformation during which we are severely challenged in every manner in order to help us see our need to decisively manage our personal energy.

These present trials and tribulations are to serve as a wakeup call to humanity. We have long seen ourselves as helpless victims, unworthy of Divine love. We have been afraid to admit to having and using divine and personal power because we don't want to be thought of as arrogant. Yet, we have the very essence of the Creator within us and we are expected to be stewards of this power—not to live in self-abasement. We are so much more than we have realized. As we are releasing our personal limitations, we are learning how to use the power of our thoughts and feelings to purposefully create the peaceful world we have been dreaming of.

Part of the goal of ascension is to recognize our oneness with each other and the planet that supports our life. Everything we do matters to the planet and humanity. Energy flows in us, between us, among us as a human family; therefore, what goes on in one part of the world is felt in all parts of the world. The air we breathe today is the same air someone on the other side of the world will breathe tomorrow. Purpose, meaning, connection, and well-being comes from inside our hearts (emotions) and minds.

Unfortunately, our pursuit of happiness through material possessions has created a "disposable" society that is damaging Mother Earth and all Her inhabitants. Almost every product on the market—especially electronics—is designed to either become obsolete or unusable within a short period of time. Offering these products at a low price makes it less expensive to purchase a replacement product rather than repair the old device. Where do these used products go? Rather than being recycled, most are placed in landfills or dumped into the oceans, where they produce toxins that end up in our soil, air, and water. Additionally, we have destroyed rainforests, polluted our air by using combustible energy to power our vehicles, and continue to deplete our natural resources.

Mother Earth is a living being with Her own consciousness. The cleansing She is doing through natural disasters is in response to the destruction and devastation we have subjected Her to. The new paradigm will include a global effort to better care for the planet that sustains human, animal, and plant life.

How Earth's Expansion Affects Humans

Everything seems to be speeding up, including soul development *Conc*
and the ascension process. In each lifetime, we typically make small
strides in reaching the next level of consciousness. Barbara
Marciniak noted in her book, *Path of Empowerment*, that we are
now evolving so quickly it is like living thousands of years in only
twenty-five. It's like having hundreds of lifetimes all rolled into one.
As you resolve your own karma (and stop creating more) and let go
of fear-based beliefs, you will start to ascend to new levels or
realms of purer and more loving consciousness.

Many repressed issues from our shadow side are emerging to be
healed and integrated. Emotionally, many people are going through
a dark night of the soul where it feels like their lives are falling
apart; people report that they have anxiety/panic attacks and feel
helpless, depressed, or angry. The dark night of the soul is intended
to create a personal shift or transformation in the way a person
approaches life. Naturally, this brings changes as the oversoul is
urging the embodied soul to make positive changes.

Even in the midst of this chaos, you may feel power rising within
you; you may be changing the way you think about yourself, the
way you manage money or make a living, who you are in a
relationship with, and where you live. You may be contemplating
more 180-degree turns.

Darkness (lower vibrations) is rising to the surface because it
cannot exist at an accelerated frequency where there is only love
and light. Things done in secret are being exposed and purged so
that we can begin to live more authentically.

Purer vibration means having a purer conscious. You may be   *Conc.*
revisiting issues from your past that you thought you had resolved.
You may have dealt with an issue as deeply as you could (or were
willing to) at the time. Things seemed stable and clear as the "mud"
settled to the bottom of the proverbial glass of water. Now the
mud is getting stirred up again and things look murky.

When you feel frustrated (as I have many times), try to remind yourself that the process of ascension is simply flushing all the impurities completely out of the glass so that only pure water remains. You haven't done anything wrong just because you are experiencing illness or feeling emotionally unstable or mentally jumbled at times. Avoid analyzing the whys and wherefores. Instead, focus on seeing yourself as the perfect soul that you already are.

Because we are so divinely connected to Source and one another, we are picking up the thoughts, feelings, and energy of those around us in an effort to heal others and help them ascend. Yet, when we still have lower vibrating energy such as resentment, fear, judgment, prejudice, a sense of entitlement or victimhood, and unhealed emotional pain within us, we easily begin to vibrate at the frequency of the energy that is being released by another person. This is known as resonation or entrainment.

The key here is to notice when you are picking up detrimental energy and continue to persevere. As you shift into purer thought and emotion, you will naturally let go of anything that is not of the light. You will finally reach a point where you are clean, clear, and aligned with purer (less dense) expansive vibrations and frequencies of Light and Love, and there will be nothing for discordant or dark energy to attach to. Thus, you will live authentically in a state of conscious awareness having purity of thought.

In addition to an increase in energetic sensitivity, our chakras are opening up and psychic and spiritual gifts are coming forth. We are hearing and seeing in other dimensions or realms. We intuitively know when someone is lying to us, we are becoming healers, we are channeling our higher selves and ascended masters, and we are sharing information to help others get free in order to make the shift. These are just some of the changes we are witnessing.

Numerology and the Shift

As I write this portion of this book, it is November 9, 2011 and the energy of 11/11/11 is being keenly felt by a lot of people. Many have been seeing double digits—especially 11 for the past two years. People have reported seeing the number 1 repeated on car tags and odometers, or that they look at a clock at exactly 11:11. This synchronicity has increased since September of 2011. The winter solstice of Dec 21, 2012 marks the end of the Mayan long count cycle. This occurs at 11:11 universal time (on the prime meridian at Greenwich). Interestingly, if you add the numbers of the date 12-21-2012 the sum is 11.

The number 11 represents new beginnings/cycles, synchronicity, the opening of portals or gateways, fresh ways of thinking, increased spiritual tendencies, and compassion. Eleven is one of the master numbers. When the number 11 is repeated, it has even more significance and is meant to call our attention to something going on spiritually, astrologically, individually, and planetary. It is a sign that something is about to change or shift.

The year 2012 is noted as the closing of a great cycle within the complex calendar system of the Mayan civilization. The ancient Mayan people of Central America (specifically the Yucatan Peninsula) were astronomically advanced and kept as many as twenty different calendars marking cyclical events with pinpoint accuracy or noting schedules for anything from seed planting and religious rites, to solar and lunar eclipses. The Mayans perceived time to be cyclical rather than linear; so, they expected events to repeat themselves in some fashion.

The Mayans indicated that the time period in which we are now in would be a time of environmental chaos (floods, fire, wind, and earthquakes), social upheaval, as well as a time of great spiritual opportunity in which humans could choose to move into a new harmonious age. The Mayans prophesied the return of Kulkukan, and modern-day Christians herald the return of Jesus Christ, also known as Lord Maitreya.

One calendar, known as the 13-Baktun or long count system, runs for just over 5,125 years. That cycle is set to complete on the winter solstice of 2012 at 11:11 Universal Time. Many people see this "end of the cycle" as the end of the world. Since the Earth has undergone many shifts that nearly wiped out the global population, some people fear that this might occur again in our near future. We don't have to look far to see that things on the Earth are rapidly changing. But, does this mean that the Earth is about to be destroyed? I hardly think so. We are on the threshold or beginning of something wonderful and peaceful. If you look at the number 11, you can imagine two upright poles side by side. This could represent a door post or portal. I like to think of it as you and me—everyone on the planet—standing side by side in unity and oneness. We really are one.

The December 21, 2012 date was considered important to the ancient tribes of the Amazon jungles, the builders of the pyramids in Egypt, indigenous people of Canada, and the Hopi Indians. As I mentioned before, the Earth is entering alignment with the equator of the Milky Way Galaxy. On this date, the Earth is also completing one full astrological cycle known as the "precession of the equinoxes" as it does approximately every 26,000 years. During this cycle, the Earth passes through each of the twelve signs of the zodiac, each lasting for 2,000–2,152 years. When all these converge, we know that something big is on Earth's horizon.

The element of surprise is best appreciated when it comes to holiday gifts and birthday parties! Sudden and unprovoked change in one's life is scary and unsettling. When people are provided with knowledge—especially when it has to do with major life changes and a significant spiritual transformation—they tend to calm down. Putting things into perspective brings comfort and we can more easily relax and go with the flow. If someone holds the belief that the changes we are experiencing means that the Earth is about to be destroyed, one will feel panic and out of control of one's own life. If a person understands that the turmoil of the shift is simply a step of progress in our spiritual evolution, he or she may be more inclined to tune in to what Spirit is saying and find peace in the process.

As far as what 2012 may bring—whether it be a catastrophic pole shift that historians and archaeologists say the Earth has experienced in the past, or an ascension out of duality thinking—if we know we are eternal souls moving from one age to another, we can rest assured that we will continue to exist *somewhere*. We will continue to have consciousness in some realm of our vast and exciting multiverse, even if it is not on planet Earth. I choose to see the glass half full rather than half empty, so my perspective on what the winter solstice of 2012 might bring is very positive.

So, are we living in the last days? Or is this just the end of one age and the beginning of another? Will the Earth be destroyed? Religions and ancient prophecies would have us think so. Mayans and other indigenous peoples have spoken of tumultuous times at the end of the age. There are signs to let us know when we are approaching the "last days" or latter phase of duality. The signs listed below come from Matthew 24: 6-14, which states that after these things the "end" shall come.

- Wars and civil unrest
- Nation rising against nation
- Famines, pestilences, earthquakes all over the Earth
- Intense hatred of others
- Offence to and betrayal of one another
- False religions and prophets that teach separation and deceive many from knowing their oneness with God
- Increased crime and violence

You could put a check mark by all of those characteristics that define our current world.

Does the "end" mean a destruction of the Earth as the Bible indicates in Matthew 24: 15-26? This text refers to other times that the Earth has been destroyed, which perhaps accounts for the mysterious disappearance of ancient civilizations such as the Mayans, Atlanteans, and Lemurians.

Archeologists have found evidence of planetary destruction that occurred as a result of either colliding with a huge foreign object or a magnetic pole shift. If suchthat were to happen again, we would be doing or experiencing the following:

- Looking for a leader who could help us survive as a species
- Fleeing into the mountains
- Running for our lives without taking anything from home— nothing but the clothes on our backs
- Wishing we had never given birth to children who have to face this calamity
- Mourning the death of many
- Dealing with harsh weather conditions and hardships
- Worrying about the survival of life on Earth as we dispose of corpses and carcasses
- Having concern because comets/meteorites, brown stars, and other foreign bodies are too near the Earth
- The sun being darkened by heavy clouds of smoke from volcanic or atomic eruptions

In her book, *Catastrophobia: The Truth Behind Earth Changes in the Coming Age of Light,* Barbara Clow Hand pinpoints that the flood of Noah occurred as little as 11,500 years ago. She says the fear of living through such a planet-wide horror is still stuck in human memory. As we see all these things occurring in the list from the Matthew reference above, we know that the time is near when Heaven and Earth *as we know it* shall pass away. Even though some people are speculating that another cataclysmic event might occur in 2012, Christ consciousness is arising in humanity and is removing the illusion of duality, linear time, and separatist thinking.

When Old Testament prophets gave a doomsday message, it was given with the hope that humanity would change in order to avoid "wrath." I believe that a huge intervention is occurring with the help of ascended masters. They are among us now in light bodies (sometimes appearing as humans), helping us shift our consciousness and behavior. If you believe in extraterrestrials, angels, and other celestial beings as I do, then you know it is possible that the Earth could be saved or at least some inhabitants rescued or "raptured" into another dimension.

> And he shall judge among the nations . . . and they shall beat their swords into plowshares, and their spears into pruninghooks: nation shall not lift up sword against nation, neither shall they learn war any more.
>
> ~ Isaiah 2:4

I believe our future is up to us. Throughout history we've been looking for a super-hero, a savior, or someone to rescue us from our own self-destruction as a race of humans. We've failed to realize that we create our own reality through our thoughts, feelings, attitudes, and behaviors. Therefore, we are the ones we've been waiting for. We're the ones who must lay down our devastating weapons of personal destruction and collective warfare and pick up the plowshare of peace. We must return to the basics of living a wholesome life in tune with Mother Earth. To see a non-violent world in which the wolf lies down with the lamb, we must stop treating humans and animals as commodities. We must become what we want to see in the world, and then demonstrate it.

I like what Anastasia says about the power of collective thought. In Book 1 of the *Ringing Cedars*

> These dimensions (of time and distance) cannot be measured by metres or seconds, but by the degree of one's conscious awareness and will. The purity of the thoughts, feelings, and perceptions held by the majority is what determines the place of humanity in time and the Universe.
>
> ~ Vladimir Megre, Anastasia

Series Vladimir Megré states on behalf of Anastasia: "If a single individual wanted a second sun to flare up in the sky, it would not appear. Things are arranged this way so that planetary catastrophes do not happen. But if everybody together wanted a second sun, it would appear." She also said, "These dimensions (of time and distance) cannot be measured by metres or seconds, but by the degree of one's conscious awareness and will. The purity of the thoughts, feelings, and perceptions held by the majority is what determines the place of humanity in time and the universe."

The quickening stage for unprecedented change is over. The Earth and humanity are already in labor and we are about to give birth to something beautiful and wonderful. Going through the birth process is not pleasant for those who resist the unfolding and opening of the portal that will lead us into a new reality. Those who have integrated accelerated frequencies in a human body are like midwives, who have come to help us take our first breath as we ascend into our light body. We are birthing the New Heaven and New Earth. We are about to understand what being *born again* really means.

> The wolf shall dwell with the lamb, the leopard shall lie down with the kid; the calf and the young lion shall abide together; the cow and the bear shall feed, the lion shall eat straw like the ox (no meat), and a little child shall lead them. They shall not hurt nor destroy in all my holy mountain.
>
> ~ Isaiah 11:6-9 paraphrased by the author

Chapter 2 ~ Ascension and the Shift

The terms oneness and awakening are being used interchangeably for the spiritual evolutionary process referred to as "ascension." Conscious evolution involves anchoring the higher energy frequencies into the physical body as well as the integration of our soul. This is occurring in the midst of some huge changes on Earth.

The expansion and acceleration of Earth's vibration has been occurring over many centuries but the shift became very noticeable in early 2011. By late autumn of that year, many people reported feeling more calm. This is most likely due to all the spiritual efforts people were making toward cleansing their own karma and bringing in and anchoring the accelerated frequencies of 11-11-11.

What is this accelerated energy that we are supposed to be integrating? What does ascension mean? How will the Earth and humanity look once the shift into purer consciousness is complete? These are some questions I will attempt to answer in this chapter.

> Ascension isn't necessarily about going "up;" it's about joining with the highest spiritual realm and connecting it with Earth. . . People need to understand that they don't leave the planet when they ascend. It can happen and some have done it.
>
> ~ Kelemeria Myarea Elohim

First, let me remind you that there are no "good" or "bad" frequencies; everything is energy. There are waves and particles, light and sound, fast and slow vibrations, dense and expanded states. Accelerated energy is a faster vibrating and very intense cosmic energy coming from the central sun. It is having a tremendous effect upon the earth, humans, and animals.

The purpose for the ascension is to raise our soul's vibration in order to ascend into higher realms of consciousness where we may enjoy oneness with our creator. In order to do this, we must get free of karma or anything unlike love that has accumulated in our field, mind, emotions, or body. Like a bride preparing for her marriage ceremony, we are here on Earth to develop our soul so that we can contain exalted vibrations, allowing us to enjoy union with our beloved in sweet oneness. We don't have to wait to have this experience—it is available within our own heart space now (see chapter 5). The time spent in preparation will automatically generate a light body that can consciously and physically travel into other realms and dimensions.

> Can a maid forget her ornaments, or a bride her attire? yet my people have forgotten me days without number. ~ Jeremiah 2:32
>
> As the bridegroom rejoiceth over the bride, so shall thy God rejoice over thee. ~ Isaiah 62:5

What is the Ascension?

Ascension is the ability to consciously live forever in a body of light. An ascended one, who has mastered the body, mind, and emotions, does not need to die or be reborn. He or she can take on the appearance of a human (or any other form) at will. The ascension (or Great Shift as some are calling it) is a period of time in which there is an increase in the soul's vibration.

I like what Annalee Skarin states in *Beyond Mortal Boundaries*: "Death is the dreary back door entrance into the other world. It is the servant's entrance. But there is a great front door of glory for those who overcome."

You don't need to know anything about ascension or practice any spiritual work in order to ascend; we will all get there eventually.

However, such practices can be tremendously helpful in speeding things along. This is not to say that everyone will ascend together. Ascension is a personal choice we make and our free will is honored regarding this process. The entire population on Earth will probably not make this choice because most don't see themselves as spirit beings in a human body. They believe that life beyond the physical world experienced with the five senses does not exist. For those who are strongly attached to Earth drama, life may continue as it always has. They simply need more time to make the changes that will allow them to join us in the higher realms.

To define ascension, I need to first share some material on the ego because this "fallen" part of us is what we are leaving behind and ascending *from*. I'm not sure if the ego is a thought form, an entity, or both. It sure seems at times that I'm dealing with something that has a mind of its own! Some say that the ego is God experiencing Himself as something other than love. (When I use the word "God" please convert this term to whatever name you use to define the benevolent, all-knowing, all-loving source of creation, universal consciousness, or matrix of limitless energy.) I define the ego as the part of us that *believes* it is separate from Source or Spirit (God-Goddess). These fragmented parts of us were created from traumatic experiences (in this life or a previous incarnation) and/or from our acceptance of the limiting beliefs of our ancestors.

The ego (our limited self) says it wants to protect us from what it perceives as harm, but in reality it prevents us from expanding our mind and growing spiritually. It keeps us stuck in destructive patterns that secure only one thing—the continuing of a separatist mindset. The ego believes that you are separate from me and vice versa. It believes that we are separate and inferior to God rather than part of Him/Her. It believes that humans are superior to other forms of life. There is really *no way* that anyone or anything can be separate from God—the Life force, the Divine Matrix—from which all substances (souls, humans, animals, plants, stars, etc.) are created.

The separatist mindset causes us to disconnect from one another as well as from our emotions. Moving into purer consciousness means we must begin showing compassion for others, including animals and the Earth. The manner in which we have polluted the Earth is despicable. The cruel way we raise animals in factory farms and slaughter them as a food source is a sad disgrace. The writing of this book has changed me in many ways, but the most evident is that I can no longer tolerate an omnivorous diet. Animals have feelings—nerve receptors capable of feeling physical pain as well as personality and emotions. They bond with one another and form families and communities; they express sorrow whenever they encounter a loss. I began to ask myself, "Why is it justifiable to eat a farm animal but we would never eat our domesticated pet?" Based upon the Garden of Eden story, no animals died until after humans started to believe they were separate from God. I am in no way judging anyone who eats meat, but I am asking you to consider what needs to be done if we truly want a non-violent and peaceful planet. The answer seems obvious: we must end the death and suffering on our own dinner plate. Besides showing compassion for all God's creatures and being good stewards of the Earth, it's also for our own health that we return to eating the vegetation supplied by Mother Earth. If we eat what comes out of the Earth, we might be more conscious of how polluting the Earth detrimentally affects us.

Currently, the average human body is very acidic and toxic. It has been proven that the consumption of sugar, processed foods, and meat are linked to a multitude of health issues such as cardiovascular disease, diabetes, and obesity. You can help to free your body from an unhealthy state by changing to a plant-based diet that includes whole grains, fruits, nuts, vegetables, and legumes. A vegan diet is the cleanest and most efficient way to detox the body and provide high nutrition without feeling hungry or deprived. It also lowers cholesterol, lowers blood pressure, prevents osteoporosis, and reduces the risk of heart disease, cancer, and stroke. It takes wise planning, advanced preparation, and an investment of your time and energy to eat in this fashion, but aren't you and your body worth it? Our bodies are the temple of the Holy Spirit!

Recognizing our oneness with everything is a vital part of the integration process. When faced with worry of any kind we can recognize our fearful thoughts as part of the programming that must be undone. This programming may have resulted from a traumatic experience in which some part of the psyche hid or broke away because it either felt unsafe or bravely stepped into a protector role. These disenfranchised soul particles may have been brought in from a previous lifetime. Or they may have appeared when we bought into the fear-based thinking that was handed down to us from our parents, church, or society—in this lifetime or another. Regardless of when or how they occurred, these fragmented aspects of our soul are simply performing the role we assigned to them.

Ascension comes after the resurrection of the Christ within us. There can be no resurrection until something (the ego, beliefs in separateness) dies. This is why we encounter opportunities for great spiritual growth during the dark night of the soul and other heartbreaking events. The reason why the purification path to ascension has been so difficult is because we have resisted the process that brings an end to suffering and dethrones the ego. It is very important for us to recognize the cleansing that is occurring so we can consciously participate in this purification process.

So, whenever we are moving to the next stage of spiritual evolution, we may reach a "ceiling" or resistance. The dismantling of this energetic barrier is a very deceptive process because the more we resist it, the stronger it gets in its effort to distract us and pull our attention away from our goal of oneness. The temptation to fight the ego is strong, and ironically it is in this "struggle" that we gain the strength to push through the elusive ceiling of separatism. Because whatever we place emphasis on will increase, the victory over the ego is more quickly accomplished by refusing to engage in the battle it offers. The answer then is to focus on the Divine essence within the Sacred Heart, which raises your vibration.

Enjoy your spiritual practice, and maintain your own energy rather than setting up fortresses to protect against external forces. I address this more in depth in Chapter 5 under the subheading Mental Thoughts.

How the Ascension Looks

Those who have read my other books know that I come from a fundamentalist religious background; I was a church pianist and intercessor (prayer warrior) for most of my life prior to 1999. Even though I no longer believe in the legalistic gloom and doom of the Judeo-Christian text, I do reference Bible passages because this text has such an influence upon Western belief systems.

Using a Bible reference as an analogy, we humans are the prodigal son returning home after squandering our riches, giving away our sacred power, and forgetting that we are divine beings. The ascension is the process of homecoming. Ascension brings about restitution in all life forms on Earth. For the human form, this may very well cause shifts in the DNA that will allow for the new cellular structure of the light body. So, if I had to describe how the final work of ascension would look, I would say humans (some, but perhaps not all) would reside in a restructured light body that is able to bi-locate, disappear in one place and reappear in another, and travel from this carbon-based planet to other dimensions. The seven primary (and secondary) karmic patterns of Earth would be non-existent or barely operable if the majority of humans choose to ascend. As a result, once the ascension is complete, there would be no sickness, death, suffering, or loss of any kind. Since there would be nothing to fear in this Utopia; the ego—driven by fear—would not be a problem because we would be operating from a place of pure love. Perhaps this is the new Heaven and new Earth described in Revelation 21: 1-4 of the Bible.

And I saw a new heaven and a new earth: for the first heaven and the first Earth were passed away; and there was no more sea. And I John saw the holy city, New Jerusalem, coming down from God out of heaven, prepared as a bride adorned for her husband. And I heard a great voice out of heaven saying, Behold, the tabernacle of God is with men, and he will dwell with them, and they shall be his people, and God himself shall be with them, and be their God. And God shall wipe away all tears from their eyes; and there shall be no more death, neither sorrow, nor crying, neither shall there be any more pain: for the former things are passed away...

The writer of this passage of scripture was said to have been taken into the future by an angel to see that great city descending out of heaven, possibly suspended in another dimension. According to Isaiah 65:17 (a cross reference to Revelation 21) humans will not remember how things used to be. Hopefully, the physical Earth will not be destroyed as indicated in the quote above.

Whether in this galaxy or in another universe, there is a realm of existence where death, sickness, and suffering do not occur. There is no violence or fear of robbery or loss. The only thing that keeps us from manifesting this type of existence in the Earth plane is fear, which is the opposite of love; we allow fear to erect a wall that blinds us and keeps us from seeing how powerful we really are. The more we dismantle this wall or veil, the more we will connect to that heavenly vision and realize that we are the ones who are creating whatever reality we encounter. Removing these hindrances is done through purification practices, such as the exercises listed in Chapter 5, that bring us back to oneness.

Thoughts on Immortality

As I first began to ponder the ascension, I was drawn to consider why things currently on Earth die and why it is possible to shift our mindset to create physical immortality on this planet. Those who are psychically aware of other dimensions know that the soul is immortal and lives on in a spiritual body after the physical body dies; like me, many others have interacted with the spirits of the "deceased" several times. I have a hard time believing that a benevolent creator would create death, war, hatred, greed, manipulation, destruction, or anything that fades away, dies, or perishes. Perishable things exist because they are part of the limitless possibilities available to us as co-creators. Like a veil drawn over human consciousness in the proverbial Garden of Eden, we created the illusion of separation and it became part of 3-D Earth reality. This "fall from oneness" is also known as *the curse* in the Bible. Humans then began to experience death of the physical body, which prior to that time had been immortal. There is no mention of death until the first animal was slain to provide clothing for the humans, who began to see themselves as separate from or abandoned and punished by God. Thus, a picture of death was inserted on top of the picture of life that was already in the photo frame of the human experience. We see this picture of death every day, but the image of immortal life is still behind the scenes for anyone who is willing to look behind the veil.

Humans had not created anything prior to this time—they only enjoyed what God had created. Therefore, nothing was labeled as bad—it was all good. This curse, which affected the entire Earth: plants, animals, humans, etc. opened to humans a full range of possibilities in the Earth plane. Thanks to this "fall," we

> Whosoever believeth in him should not perish, but have eternal (immortal) life.
>
> ~ John 3:15

became aware that we could use energy such as thoughts, intentions, and emotions to create, see, or experience anything we want. Having free will and feeling inferior to God, humans chose to create from a limiting mindset. Because our thoughts, beliefs, feelings, attitudes, and words are the materials used to manifest or create our reality, we brought death upon our planet.

The Bible is not silent concerning immortality and enhanced longevity. We read about many people who lived longer than we now do—even with our current medical knowledge and technological intervention in near-death crises. Genesis 5:8 states, "And all the days of Seth were nine hundred and twelve years, and he died." While this sounds impossible, it's not that farfetched. The body has the ability to constantly reproduce perfect cells and keep the body in perfect health. Some people mentioned in the Bible did not die at all. Elijah was whisked away in a chariot of fire, possibly a UFO or his light body (2 Kings 2:11 and Ezekiel 1:4-26).

The soul is already immortal. The body *can* be. Death is eternal life *without* your body. Ascension is eternal life *with* your physical body. If you are attempting to ascend you must realize that your body is going with you into the higher realms (sometimes called the afterlife). In order to do this, the body must vibrate at a faster rate, lose density, and become spirit matter.

Master Saint Germain gave this message in *Unveiled Mysteries* (authored by Godfré Ray King): "Eternal Youth is the Flame of God abiding in the body of man—the Father's Gift of Himself to His Creation. Youth and beauty of both mind and body can only be kept *permanently* by those individuals who are strong enough to shut out discord, and whoever does that can and will express Perfection and maintain it." So much for all those anti-aging creams! The fountain of youth is not in a jar or tube; it's contained in our thoughts and feelings! As we rack up Earth years, we accumulate detrimental energy when we do not diligently guard our hearts (feelings/emotions). We must refuse to entertain thoughts or feelings of judgment, fear, worry, or anything unlike love.

During a physical lifetime, a human being that attains the state of immortality is called an ascended master. He or she has mastered or overcome the cycle of death and rebirth (reincarnation) by perfecting themselves through spiritual purification practices, which removed all their karma. Below, I will mention some who have achieved immortality:

- In Buddhist history quite a few masters have achieved this, and the master who is most well-known for this achievement is Guru Rinpoche, who is still living today.

- Enoch walked with God and was no more (Genesis 5:24)

- Mahavatar Babaji and other Indian sadhus have appeared in various bodies long after the time that most humans give up their physical bodies and embrace death. My friend, Sondra Ray, has met a woman who is more than 400 years old.

- In *Ascension Connecting with the Immortal Masters and Beings of Light*, Susan Shumsky mentions characters in the Bible who have ascended, and she names at least two dozen from cultures such as Native American, African, Eastern Indian, and Chinese.

- In the US, Annalee Skarin has disappeared in one location and reappeared in another many times in front of various audiences.

Then, why do we still have bodily death and see other living things die? Because we have not realized that we have other options such as shifting into a light body. We have not grasped the fact that dying is a choice. We commit suicide on a daily basis through the choices we make and the thoughts we hold as truth. The belief that death is inevitable is a huge collective thought form that I compare to a snowball rolling downhill, gathering more material as it descends. If only a few who read this book will start challenging their own beliefs (we can't change others—we can only influence them), we can start leveling the ground so the snowball slows down. Then, as more people start embracing their immortality, we will see the snow ball as the fluffy stuff or illusion that it really is. It's time to remember and practice empowered options.

> For the law of the spirit of life in Christ Jesus hath made me free from the law of sin and death [the law of karma] ... The spirit of him that raised up Jesus from the dead dwells in you, and he that raised up Christ from the dead shall also quicken your moral bodies by his spirit that dwelleth in you.
>
> ~ Romans 8:2-11

Why Did Jesus Die?

The question came up during my research for this book: Why did Jesus die? Certainly he knew that immortality is an option. There is

42

some speculation as to whether or not his body actually died. He is reported to have been adept at suspended animation—the slowing of breath, heartbeat, and involuntary functions that cause the eyes to be distant and fixed and the entire body to become cold and stiff as if dead. It appears that the body is dead; however, the body does not decay while awaiting the return to life. This is done by fully mastering the mind, emotions, and body. Nevertheless, let's say that Jesus did die. What would be the purpose? This great teacher demonstrated that death in our physical body *can* be overcome. According to the scriptures, Jesus died for (because of, or as a result of) our sins (the fear-based belief in separation from God-Goddess). He set a powerful example of non-violence, non-resistance, and how to respond whenever we feel attacked.

Jesus said that the last thing to be conquered is death. Since the soul already had eternal life when Jesus came to Earth 2,000 years ago, the death to be conquered is regarding that of the physical body. The first thing to be conquered is our mind! The mind and emotions produce results in the body. If physical death came as a result of man's thoughts (that the body *should* deteriorate) then, the resurrection of the dead (immortality) can be achieved by a change in our collective beliefs. For whatever we think about, we bring about. The mind can create sustained health and life to the body because the body follows the deepest beliefs we hold in our minds.

If we want to change the death "urge," we will collectively have to start believing in immortality of the body and stop unconsciously committing slow suicide with our thoughts. The wide-spread experience of immortality may or may not happen in this current generation and it may not occur for everyone—again, choice and free will are honored—but we have to start somewhere. We can begin by deciding to dearly love and care for our body, and consciously use our mind and emotions to strengthen the life urge and put away all thoughts that keep the death urge intact. The answer is to stop believing in separation and live as Jesus did—as one with God. The spiritual purification we practice will not be in vain. It will produce results and a shift in the collective consciousness of humanity.

What is a Merkaba?

Everyone has a merkaba (also spelled merkabah) or electro-magnetic energy field (aura) that surrounds the body. It is the multi-dimensional vehicle that our consciousness resides in and from which we draw physical, emotional, mental, and spiritual energy. Consisting of two equally sized, interlocked tetrahedra (one points up and the other down), the merkaba resembles a Star of David inside a circle.

Comprised of three words: Mer (light that spins like wheels within itself), Ka (spirit) and Ba (body), in ancient Egypt merkaba meant a rotating field of light that serves as an inter-dimensional gateway to take the spirit and the body from one world to another. In the Hebrew language the loose translation is "to ride in God's chariot," which reminds me of Elijah's ascension mentioned in 2 Kings 2:10-13. The merkaba needs to be activated in order to spin properly (to resemble a saucer) and allow all of the light body to stabilize in the human body and expand into the next set of dimensional fields of existence and progressively ascend.

One note about the multidimensional planes of existence: Jesus referred to them as "many mansions," which shows us that there are other life forms co-existing in many different dimensions.

What is a Light Body?

The human body will need to take a different form in order to transcend this third-dimensional level of existence. A crystaline structure that uses light, rather than food and water, as a fuel source is called a light body. There is a lot of emphasis placed upon the eternality of the soul in traditional churches, but not a lot of emphasis is placed on the resurrection body. However, this "glorified" body is mentioned frequently in the Bible. The light body is less dense than a physical body and is the spiritual body that the soul manifests in the afterlife (think apparition). I believe that it is possible to shift into a light body without having the physical body die, and that an ascended soul can take on the likeness/appearance of any human body at any age he or she has been in other incarnations. I base this belief upon the way Jesus' followers had difficulty recognizing Him when He appeared to them in His light body. When He appeared to Mary, she thought He was a gardener (John 20:14-15) until He spoke to her. In Luke 24:13-32, He walked and talked with two of His disciples on the road to Emmaus, and they did not realize it was Him until later when He broke the bread. When He called to the disciples, who were in a boat, they did not recognize Him in John 21:4.

After his resurrection, Jesus was seen in His light body by more than 500 people at one time after He resurrected his physical body. Jesus also appeared in His light body many times while incarnated on Earth. He was in His light body when He came walking on the troubled seas toward His disciples, who thought He was a ghost. In I Corinthians 15, Paul is said to have had an epiphany in which he saw Jesus in His light body. In Mark 9, Jesus met with Moses and Elias, and was transfigured on a high mountain. There, His clothing started shining, whiter than anything on Earth. I find it interesting that Jesus told them that some who were present at that meeting would not taste of death until they had seen the kingdom of God (the New Heaven and New Earth) come with power. Did they see the Kingdom of God in their lifetime? Are they still living among us in carbon-based form? Are they in their light body manifesting as needed? Are they now ascended masters guiding us from behind the veil? Food for thought.

Hariakhan "Babaji" Maharaj is a mahavatar (a human able to materialize a body at will) who goes by many names. Babaji is said to have been alive for thousands of years, dwelling in caves in the Himalayas. Nobody knows when or where he was born. Appearing and disappearing suddenly, he was seen by many people in the 19th and 20th centuries. In a holy cave at the foot of Kumaon Mount Kailash at Haidakhan in India between 1970 and 1984 Babaji was seen primarily as a young man about eighteen to twenty years of age; yet, his appearance varied even when he was observed by several people simultaneously in different places. Witnesses reported that Babaji had great physical strength but ate very little food. He never slept, walked fast, and conversed in whatever language he was addressed. Like Jesus, Babaji performed miracles to alleviate the suffering at hand. But mostly, people are drawn to him because of the bliss they experience in his presence. Several people, including Guru Charnasrit and Baba Hari Dass, have written about him, but the most popular work is *Autobiography of a Yogi* written by Paramahansa Yogananda.

Might you and I expect to be able to appear in a light body similar to Jesus and Babaji? The light body is our true form. We are transcending into our light body and I believe we will soon start doing even greater works than Jesus did, and this includes being able to bi-locate or dematerialize in one location and reappear in another. I think of Philip, who was miraculously "caught away" by the Spirit after helping an Ethiopian man riding in a chariot understand the scripture he was reading (Acts 8:39). According to the Bible, corruptible flesh will put on incorruption (light body), and this mortal mindset of separation will experience immortality or oneness. From this, I conclude that it is likely that people on the planet who are now undergoing the process of ascension may not experience physical death.

> In my Father's house are many mansions: if it were not so, I would have told you. I go to prepare a place for you.
>
> ~ John 14:2

I Corinthians 15: 40-44 talks about our having two types of body: celestial (spiritual) and terrestrial (natural or of Earth material). The terrestrial body will put on incorruption and be raised to the level (vibration) of the spiritual body that can travel to multidimensional planes of existence, or what Jesus referred to as the "many mansions" in His father's house. Just because we can't see these realms with our limited spectrum of vision, doesn't mean they don't exist. I believe that we may even be living parallel lives on other levels of consciousness.

We are on the verge of something wonderful and spectacular. Signs indicate that we are on the cusp of the planetary appearing of the New Heaven and the New Earth coming down from God out of the heavens—likely suspended in an alternate dimension. The Bible and other religious texts indicate that a change at the end of time (leaving the Piscean Age and entering the Aquarian Age) may come suddenly "in the twinkling of an eye." That doesn't necessarily mean everyone will enter this new realm of consciousness. I personally believe that our free will gives us a choice about whether or not we will ascend. The Bible is not consistent about this. In one reference, it says that *everyone* will be changed. Yet, in Matthew 24:37–42, the Bible indicates that *some* will be taken up into that dimension before others and that some will be left behind.

> *But as the days of Noah were, so shall also the coming of the Son of man be. For as in the days that were before the flood they were eating and drinking, marrying and giving in marriage, until the day that Noe [Noah] entered into the ark, And knew not until the flood came, and took them all away; so shall also the coming of the Son of man be. Then shall two be in the field; the one shall be taken, and the other left. Two women shall be grinding at the mill; the one shall be taken, and the other left. Watch therefore: for ye know not what hour your Lord doth come.*

To grow spiritually is to have full awareness of love for one's self, others, all physical life, and the Earth and Her well-being. If a person is not interested in spiritual growth and does not want to ascend, he or she probably won't notice that things are shifting for others. But for those who are shifting and assisting others in their ascension process, they will eventually be caught up together in the New Heaven and New Earth. How exciting!

The Effects of Ascension

Ascension brings about the expansion of our auric field, chakras, subtle bodies, merkaba, and the etheric body that surrounds the Earth and all Her life forms. You've witnessed the Earth's response to this expansion. The choice to ascend brings about a restoration of whatever has become diseased in the physical body. I see humans responding both positively and negatively to the fragmented parts of us such as sickness, death, negative thoughts, discordant emotions, and limiting fear-based beliefs that are coming up to be integrated with the light. There's no need to worry if your body is sick that it cannot ascend. Ascension can occur after death (as it did for Jesus).

As an empath, you may be a forerunner waking up ahead of other people. Perhaps you went through a dark night of the soul years ago and cleared a lot of the effects of the seven karmic patterns of Earth and any negative issues stored in cellular memory from this and other lifetimes. As you continue to expand and "lighten up," you are discovering your purpose for being on Earth during such tumultuous times.

It's likely that you have a burning desire to help others transcend their karmic limitations. For some time now, you may have been sensing subtle shifts in the energy around you. Since your awareness has accessed other dimensions of consciousness, you may feel, sense, hear, or smell things that those around you do not.

I've heard some say they are seeing brilliant colors that have never been seen on Earth before. Some seem to know when something is about to happen. You may be able to tell when someone is lying to you, or know secrets that another person has have not disclosed to you. Perhaps you have creativity, talents, and skills opening up that you have not studied. Some who have been teased about being the "sensitive one in the family" are now being looked to for strength and guidance.

As you have parts of yourselves awakened, you may feel a little overwhelmed. These changes may leave you asking the question:

Who am I? You may even feel that you are no longer the person you once were. If you have experienced peculiar occurrences like these, you are not alone. You are being affected by these changes because we are all one in spirit and when one heals, we all heal.

Working with Ascended Masters

Each embodied soul needs an anchor in higher realms of consciousness to stabilize the vibration of the physical body on Earth. We wear the vibrational frequencies of those we align with, and naturally the purer, the more enjoyable. Some people are now working with ascended masters to help the Earth and humanity shift into lighter planes of consciousness. They are receiving intense and pure energy in their bodies in order to anchor these frequencies in the Earth plane.

In allowing ascended masters to send pure frequencies of energy from cosmic, solar, and multidimensional sources, a number of fully-trained empaths are using their chakras and subtle bodies as channels similar to high-voltage transformers, which step down intensely vibrating frequencies into a more useable and less harmful current that can be accepted by humanity. However, this is causing some emotional, mental, and physical discomfort. In addition to trying to heal their *own* past, these people may feel drained because they are picking up negative energy from those around them in order to transmute it and free others from karma and suffering. Karma is the "law of sin and death" that the Bible mentions. It keeps us on a cycle of reincarnation, which is a very slow way to ascend.

> For the wages of sin [living in separation/ego] is death, but the gift of God is eternal [immortal] life through Christ.
>
> ~ Romans 6:23

Many starseeds (souls who have been to other places before coming to Earth), walk-ins (souls that come into a mature body rather than being born into an infant), lightworkers (evolving souls here to help the planet ascend), and indigos (children who possess unusual and/or supernatural traits or abilities) have agreed to come to Earth to perform certain duties.

Assisting souls who are incarnating into the Earth or crossing over into the afterlife has been a duty of mine for a long time, but it took me years of suffering with the detrimental energy of some departing and/or earthbound souls before I learned what was going on and how to manage this task.

Some of you are using energy, light, and information to heal people, plants, animals, and the Earth's soil, air, and water. Some of you are serving as activists for social reform, humanitarian efforts, and better health/living conditions throughout the world. Others have discovered a talent for writing and teaching, delivering channeled messages, or providing intuitive readings. Some are finding that they can influence the weather, align the earth's gridlines (ley lines), and do many other important spiritual tasks such as transmuting karma for others.

Transmuting Karma for Others

In order for the Earth to ascend, we have to deal with the detrimental energy stuck in the astral body. According to Ethan Vorly, the unresolved karma or crystallization of a lifetime is housed in the astral body that surrounds the physical human body. He says that if someone dies and is not cremated, the energy accumulated in the astral body remains in the Earth plane where it can affect other people as it awaits the former soul's return to an Earth body to claim it (in utero or childhood) and pick up where it left off. If there is enough dense (slow-vibrating) energy in the astral body it can stabilize to the point that it takes on persona and a plasma-like structure (See http://www.entityclearing.com).

Those who are in an Earth body naturally have brought in energetic imprints (karma) from past lives. We also generate more during our current incarnation if we are not practicing spiritual purification. These experiences are recorded in the Akashic Records also known as the Book of Life in the Bible. This is the stuff that makes us feel so bad, even as we are allowing it to be transmuted while forming more authentic and healthy patterns. Ascended masters and those on purer planes of consciousness are available to assist us in the process of personal clearing as well as helping us serve as conduits to transmute negativity for others. Many empathic people do this without a clue as to why they cry when others cry, feel sick when someone they love is ill, or absorb the detrimental energy of their environment in order to neutralize it.

In my book, *Whose Stuff is This?*, I mentioned that we should not take on the task of transmuting the negativity and pain of others. I still think it is best to allow others to learn the lessons their souls have setup in the experiences they encounter. However, it has come to my awareness that some souls are in body now for the exact purpose of transmuting the suffering of others to help them "catch up" in the ascension process. You should not use your physical body for this task. Instead of using your lower chakras for clear sensing/feeling to glean information, use your upper chakras (particularly the third eye, which is the sixth chakra located between your eyebrows) to get a clear knowing and vision about the work that needs to be done. This method accesses the faster-vibrating energy of the spirit realm rather than your physical body and the slower vibrating energy of the Earth plane to transmute. Personally, I call upon ascended master St. Germain to bring his violet flame of transmutation to neutralize and transform detrimental energy into beneficial energy. I've been doing this for many years and it works great!

Because this transmutation mission is something agreed to before incarnation, not everyone is expected to do this work. If you are a walk-in, you may have taken up residence in the body of a natal soul who left detrimental karmic imprints in the astral body.

Soul exchanges are more common than you might realize. We will discuss this in Chapter 5. These "newcomers" must take on the task of transmuting karmic patterns of the natal soul before they can fully begin their personal mission. For some empathic souls this process causes a great deal of suffering to the body they have entered. These beings bring in loving frequencies from dimensions of purer consciousness, and the human body's DNA may not be ready to manage this power surge. These beings carry the frequency from "home" or purer domains and are constantly being fed additional frequencies from their galactic companions and ascended masters. This intense and high-vibrating energy can't get through to the chakras when there is a lot of clutter in the auric field or in the astral or other subtle bodies. Or, if the energy does manage to get in, it can act like an ungrounded electrical current that jolts the body, mind, and emotions of the recipient. Understandably, this can be disturbing in many ways. Thus, it is very important to help them adjust so they can set about doing the mission they were sent to do. You may very well be one of these newly incarnated souls. This could be why you were led to this book. You've asked for help, right?

Even if you are not called to do the work of transmutation, you can still work with ascended masters, and I highly recommend that you do. As evolving souls, we basically have all the information we need and are able to vibrate at whatever level we want. But, these cosmic beings—as well as angels, archangels, ascended masters, and other non-physical beings of light—do not infringe upon our free will or make assumptions about what we want in life. Therefore, we must ask for their help.

That doesn't mean that some of us are not unconsciously working with these masters on a soul level or perhaps during the dream state. Many empaths are becoming more aware of their multidimensional experiences. You may see, feel, hear, and sense these spiritually-advanced beings around you.

It is not just angels and guides helping us now. There are also ETs (extraterrestrials) and celestial beings from different planets and dimensions. Their spaceships are in other dimensions unseen by the normal spectrum of light detected by human eyes. However, some ships are manifesting in third dimension, as we have seen a tremendous increase in UFO sightings and actual video footage of them in news reports and on YouTube. Some of those who were hushed regarding the 1947 Roswell crash that occurred in New

Mexico are coming forth with the truth about what the US Government has denied for years. Beings not of Earth origin are all around us. You may have connected with these groups during meditation or your dream state. Most are here to help the planet evolve, but before interacting with these beings, ask the same question you would ask if a disincarnated soul came to you, "Are you of the Light and are you working the Divine Plan?" They must respect your free will and will leave you alone if you tell them to go away.

Having a clear aura and open chakras helps us become more conscious of the work we are doing with spiritually-advanced beings on other levels of existence. Whether you work with these light beings consciously or unconsciously, it is helpful to assist them in assisting you and humanity by clearing space within yourself in order to hear and carry out the instructive and encouraging messages they send us.

Chapter 3 ~ What Happened to You?

In addition to the shift that the Earth is going through in raising her own vibration, there are many other things that can trigger a personal surge of ascension energy. These include, but are not limited to, having a near-death experience (including attempted suicide); practicing spiritual purification; receiving a miracle healing; undergoing a soul retrieval or past-life regression; having a walk-in or soul exchange; or merging or blending with your oversoul. Like me, you may have had more than one of these kinds of experiences.

Our souls are maturing and evolving regardless of what label we give it. At any time, we may experience a bump up in energy that takes us to a new spiritual level. The end result is we are being spiritually transformed as we seek to develop our souls. We are beginning to realize that we are one in spirit, and there is a whole lot more than what our limited human understanding and beliefs have allowed us to accept. Perhaps giving an experience a label helps define it. Realizing that I had been through a soul exchange certainly gave me new understanding and the ability to find tools to help me integrate the experience. Simply knowing what to call it pointed me in the direction to find the support I needed.

I will touch on each of these experiences in this chapter. Some of the information provided here will be from my personal experience; other parts will be from my research and stories shared by those I interviewed for this book.

Near-Death Experience

Have you ever come close to death's door only to be drawn back to your body? Prior to the 1970s no one had heard of a near-death experience (NDE). Now it is common for people to open up and share what happened to them during an event that almost took their life—or in some cases did! Thanks to medical intervention practices used today some people have been pronounced dead and then came back to life several minutes later. The stories they report in such instances are consistent: life reviews, a tunnel of light, meeting deceased loved ones, seeing ascended masters, communicating telepathically, and being sent back to their body to complete the life they started. Many of those who have an NDE say that they experienced immense peace or indescribable love, beyond anything that can be imagined in this human existence. Those who have been wrapped in this feeling and come back to tell about it may find it difficult to be here on Earth with all its sorrow.

In past centuries we have not been comfortable with admitting to having gone through events such as this. As a society, we tend to think that anything we cannot explain or experience through the five traditional senses of sight, smell, taste, touch, and hearing is not valid. The word "near-death experience" was not even in our vernacular or understanding forty or so years ago. We weren't able to accept it through our self-imposed filters of what is possible and what is not. It is now a reality talked about in mainstream media. Therefore, it has validity.

Even without people sharing publicly, the NDE was the most common experience that created a shift in a person's life and personality in the 1970s. I have had two near-death experiences in this body. My near-death experiences as well as stories of other NDE-ers are in my book, *More Than Meets the Eye ~ True Stories about Death, Dying, and Afterlife*. See deathdyingafterlife.com for more information about that book. Each NDE changed me and opened new psychic abilities and intensified my desire for spiritual pursuits. Coming back to Earth and feeling like a different person is a common report among those who have had NDEs.

Practicing Spiritual Purification

From the days of circuit-riding evangelists to modern-day energy work, an attempt to find healing and feel a connection with Spirit has had a profound influence upon seekers. From what I have experienced in typical church revivals is that the euphoria and emotional surge experienced at the event is short-lived because no real change occurs inwardly. Any vows we take to live a better life fail as soon as the ego (limited self) takes the wheel again. The change we seek must come from allowing the heart and mind of God to overwrite the fear-based thoughts of our limited self. This requires a daily effort that keeps the higher self in the driver's seat of our mind. Our efforts to turn over a new leaf rarely produce long-term results. Regularly reading and applying the concepts presented in *A Course in Miracles* has had a tremendous impact on my thought life. Whenever I feel out of sorts, this is what I turn to. I know I will be reminded of how senseless the ego's offers are. I immediately allow the Holy Spirit to replace the ludicrous thoughts in my mind with higher thoughts that bring peace, love, and joy. It works every time!

Even though our soul development is a personal undertaking with which we must be intimately and consistently involved, I certainly won't discount the value of community-based spiritual renewal events. Every summer at church camp I grew in my relationship to Spirit. As a young adult I always looked forward to revival meetings and seeing how many would get "saved" as a result of the Spirit's work. In other words, I was hungry for my own soul to grow and be healed and I wanted the same for other people.

A movement known as the "Toronto Blessing" began at the Toronto Canada Airport Vineyard Church in January 1994. This affected me in a positive manner even though the "manifestations of the Spirit" were not accepted in my home church. It opened me to a new level of awareness regarding the spirit world, prophetic signs, healing, and miracles. It displayed some wonderful supernatural phenomena that caused many people to have a shift in consciousness, personality, life habits, and true spiritual transformation.

Prayer and fasting, rebirthing, conscious breathing, and rituals in which you ask to be assisted in reaching the next level have a great effect upon soul development. When I was involved in intercessory prayer and fasted one day per week, psychic and spiritual gifts manifested in my life. Even today, each time I embark upon an effort to clear karma from my astral body, I feel a deeper connection to Spirit and undergo a process of "stripping away" things that no longer serve me. My ego and emotions always protest this process, but as I persevere, the results are always good. I feel more loving, less judgmental, and have a peaceful, more enthusiastic outlook on life.

Miraculous Healing

There's something about coming close to death or being very ill or injured that causes us to reevaluate everything in our lives. It's also hard not to change our old, limited ways of viewing life when we have a spiritual encounter that creates a miraculous healing in our body or emotions. Your spiritual transformation could have been triggered by such an event.

Many empowered souls such as Dr. Eric Pearl have partnered with light beings and energy in purer dimensions to bring healing vibration, light, and information to the Earth plane. This reconnective healing can help transmute the energy of fear, darkness, and retribution. Dr. Pearl's story about how he came to employ this "otherworldly" help is not only fascinating, it rings true to many who have suddenly been healed or became healers within the past ten years. Check out my interview with reconnection healer, Dr. Eric Pearl on *We Are One in Spirit Podcast*: http://dld.bz/aEdrb.

More and more people are learning how true healing comes from within our own body and thoughts. I especially like Dr. Susan Allison's book, *Empowered Healer*. I first learned of Susan's work when I interviewed her as a guest on my podcast (http://dld.bz/aHyN6). Many people believe they have to look outside themselves for healing but Susan teaches us how to heal ourselves by going within and partnering with the support and help of angels and spirit guides. Yet, she also advocates the use of medicine or doctors to accompany this effort—a well-rounded approach. The thing I like most about her teaching is that it is so simple that anyone can do what she recommends and experience improvement in a physical or emotional health condition. That's because true self-healing comes from self-discovery and listening to the voice within and following its directions.

"In order to get well, it is important to look at the possible reasons you have become ill, be committed to getting better, and be willing to trust the recovery process presented in this book," writes Dr. Allison. "Then, you will have faced and released the past and can move forward with confidence, believing 100 percent in your ability to heal yourself."

Soul Retrieval

As multidimensional beings and individuations of the Divine Cosmic Intelligence, our souls have multiple counterparts or aspects residing in dimensions besides this Earth plane. There is no limit to how many individual parts make up the whole of creation. Any of these soul parts can influence or assist us in our life on Earth. An embodied soul can fragment (divide and scatter) during severe trauma or if intense emotional overload occurs. An aspect of our personality may "flee the scene" or dissociate during the ordeal and go into hiding until it feels safe to return. This aspect may go into protector mode and pop up as self-sabotage anytime we experience a similar or disturbing event.

The soul fragments can be reunited with the embodied soul through a practice known as soul retrieval. For centuries, Native American shamans have practiced the art of calling home lost parts of the soul. You may hear Janice Mickel speak about shamanic soul retrieval on *We Are One in Spirit Podcast*: http://dld.bz/T43s.

My limited experience with soul retrieval in the late 1990s produced a profound sense of healing for my inner child. During the session, I relived a childhood event that I had repressed so deeply that I did not remember it for thirty-five years. This explained the confusing snippets of a traumatic "mental video" that had replayed and troubled me for many years. When the soul retrieval was complete, the replays ceased and I no longer had ill feelings toward the woman who had abused me. Finally, my mom and I understood why I had mysteriously hated this woman all my life.

Past-Life Regression

Discovering who you were or what you did in a past life can create a change in the life you are currently living. Having information that helps you understand why certain people are in your life or why some places call to you, or why particular events trigger a subtle memory can be beneficial. I have done past-life regression and found that this significantly helped me because it added beneficial information about situations and people in my life. I was able to see one particular person as innocent of the "crime" that I perceived he had done to me. Knowing that our difficulties were not a product of this incarnation, but rather of a previous one that needed to be transcended, made forgiving this person and moving on much easier. Since we are all connected, my letting go of the detrimental feelings I had toward this person produced healing in the relationships with other people we both mutually loved. If you decide to do a regression, I hope you will avoid getting distracted by what you remember about past lives. Remember to live in the now moment.

Raising of Kundalini Energy

Kundalini energy is stored at the base of your spine in the root chakra. It naturally awakens as you develop spiritually, but it can be awakened at a faster pace. Because it's a forceful and concentrated energy that quickly moves through the chakras, many experts agree that it is dangerous to have Kundalini energy rise too quickly in the body. The sudden expanded awareness can cause serious emotional and mental problems. The rise in Kundalini energy caused my family to think I was having a nervous breakdown. You may see auras and visions of non-physical beings, experience muscle pain, headaches, panic attacks, dizziness, tingling of the skin, involuntary body movement, and energy rushes throughout your body. The sudden experience of higher levels of awareness may cause mood and temperature swings, changes in sleeping or eating patterns, out of body experiences, life-like memories of past lives, and an increase in psychic activities. Most of us are doing the best we can to keep up with all the changes we are experiencing as a result of planetary ascension. We don't need to add to the drama. However, a walk-in or near-death experience or a large download of energy from your higher self can trigger the sudden rise in Kundalini energy.

Walk-ins or Soul Exchanges

Do you feel that the soul you came here with had a sudden shift? Perhaps something life-changing happened and you became another person, more evolved with a mission to heal and help humanity. You may be a walk-in.

Typically, a soul enters the human body at conception or birth, and then exits through the portal known as death. However, birth and death are *not* the only ways for a soul to enter and leave the Earth plane. Soul exchanges (walk-ins/walk-outs) happen more frequently than you might think, and I'm not sure why this seems so strange to some people; the only difference is the size and age of the body at the soul's time of entrance. Since I may write another book especially to help those who have experienced this life-changing incident, I will only give a basic overview here.

Interest in the walk-in occurrence came about in the 1970s, through the book, *Seth Speaks: The Eternal Validity of the Soul,* channeled by Jane Roberts. In 1979, a journalist named Ruth Montgomery introduced the concept of walk-ins in her book, *Strangers Among Us.* She explained that walk-ins are souls who incarnate directly into a mature physical body with the full agreement of the soul that was born into the body. In many cases, the original soul has finished its initial mission, and agrees to leave and make its body available to another soul, rather than leave through physical death. This agreement made between two souls before incarnation, allows both souls to accomplish more soul development in one Earth lifetime. The incoming soul does not need the lessons provided by infancy and childhood and can quickly move into its Earth mission. The departing soul can move on to its next mission in the afterlife. In such agreements, the soul that only has a small amount of karma or who wants to resolve a lot of karma very quickly may take the body during the formative infant and childhood years (natal soul). These years are usually very difficult because that soul has asked for a "crash course" in order to speed up the evolutionary process. This hardship may create a very strong urge to leave the body when things get really painful.

If a soul is creating an illness in the body in order to leave the Earth plane or if the natal soul's contract is complete, it makes logical sense to offer the physical body and established adult life to another soul. From a universal perspective, a soul exchange is a wise and compassionate use of "human resources" because it meets the needs of both souls and causes less trauma for the entire family. Why cause a family to grieve the loss of a loved one through physical death when another soul (more advanced) is willing to pick up where the first soul left off?

It's interesting to note that the walk-in is often the oversoul, monad, or higher self of the natal soul, which means the effect is like a download of purer (faster vibrating) energy. Family may note many sudden changes in the person's life, but because the body retains the cellular memory of its life's experiences, most families do not realize that the natal soul has left.

As the natal soul prepares to walk out, it may arrange for its exit by creating health problems, emotional issues, or an accident that causes the body to be unconscious; some souls who are extremely desperate to leave the body may even attempt suicide. Many times the transfer occurs during a near-death experience, an out-of-body experience, a dark night of the soul, or traumatic event. It can occur while the body is asleep, while in coma, during surgery, or in a period of unconsciousness. However, more and more walk-ins are coming in consciously and with memory of their soul transfer, knowing the spiritual reason for coming into the body.

Meanwhile, the walk-in soul is arranging for its incarnation. More than likely this partner soul has been serving as a guide for the natal soul, or is at least familiar with all that has occurred thus far in the incarnation. When a soul exchange takes place, the walk-in soul maintains the lower three chakras and functions of the body, and picks up where the natal soul left off. The walk-in soul brings in its own spiritual mission, vibration, and energy signature, and connects its upper four chakras to the body.

The walk-out (natal) soul may leave completely or stay in the auric field of the body to serve as a guide or overseer. Some walk-out souls enter the afterlife and have nothing more to do with the life or family they left behind. In other cases, the natal soul stays in the auric field of the body it left so it can observe and learn lessons while the new soul picks up the pieces and begins to heal the body and emotions and resolve residual karma such as the limiting beliefs that created the natal soul's desire to exit.

The incoming soul is usually part of the same oversoul or monad; on rare occasions it may be a member of another soul group entirely. Even though there is usually a great deal of compatibility between the walk-in and walk-out souls, there is often an adjustment period in which the body must acclimate to the higher vibrations of the incoming soul, which hails from a realm where there is no linear time. There is usually a period of time in which the walk-out and walk-in souls test drive their new places. This is more for the incoming soul than the one departing because it gives the walk-in soul a chance to acclimate to being in a human body, stabilize the emotions, and get familiar with the friends and family of the natal soul.

People with a restricted mindset about the limitless possibilities of the soul may doubt that such an event can occur. Yet, these same people might easily believe in a possession in which a body is overtaken by a demon or disincarnate spirit. The walk-in is an exact opposite of a demonic possession. The transfer is done with mutual consent to move both souls forward in spiritual evolution and bring a purer vibration to the Earth. Many walk-ins are very intensely focused on accomplishing their divine purpose. To help facilitate this, they exhibit healing abilities, keen psychic sensitivity, empathy, accurate intuition, and other spiritual gifts. Walk-ins, while spiritually advanced, are not better or more enlightened than other souls on the planet. They just have an insatiable desire to complete their mission to help the Earth ascend or to comfort, educate, and assist others who are struggling to manage the changes they are experiencing.

Just like NDEs in the 1970s, the concept of walk-ins came as something new and vastly different from what our reality would allow in the 1980s and 1990s when soul exchanges began to increase. More and more walk-ins are occurring as the Earth's vibration is being raised. Today, we have more walk-ins than anyone would ever guess—and many don't even know they are one! Once people know what the experience looks and feels like and enough have overcome the confusion that sometimes takes place when the event occurs, we will see this as a common experience. You may be a walk-in. You know something unexplainable happened to change your life. Could that be why you were drawn to this book?

Picking up the Pieces

If you had a soul shift or walk-in, you probably remember when you began to feel totally different. The body may have been in shock if this has happened due to a car accident, surgery, coma, near-death experience, or suicide attempt. Perhaps you did not recognize the people around you or feel a kinship with family members at first.

The morning after my walk-in occurred, I packed my bags and left a 22-year marriage; I forgot to tell my daughter goodbye or ask if she wanted to come with me. I was so confused and disoriented that I didn't even call my mom to let her know where I was until twelve hours later. Even though you retain the memories of your body's past history, you may have had lapses of memory—especially regarding your childhood. I finally asked my mother to fill in some details regarding what my childhood home looked like.

When you buy a used vehicle or house, the former owner may have left some mechanical or deferred maintenance that needs to be tended to. The same is true with walk-ins. The natal soul may have left physical or emotional messes for the walk-in soul to sort through and repair. In addition to wading through that mess, the body must deal with the influx of higher-vibrating energy that the walk-in soul emanates. It can feel like a 220-volt current moving through a circuit wired for 110 current. This amplification may cause the body's nervous system to feel as though it has been fried. Nervousness, tension, anxiety, headaches, body aches, emotional outbursts, and physical illnesses have to be worked out.

A walk-in soul inherits the cellular memory within the body. Naturally, there is a transition period during which the personality and characteristics of the original soul fade away and allow the traits and giftedness of the incoming soul to emerge. However, it is not uncommon for walk-in souls to get "stuck" in the lingering patterns of the natal soul, thus compromising the purpose and mission of the walk-in soul.

A walk-in usually occurs in mid-life, which means these souls are not faced with forms of parental discipline or educational systems that are out of alignment with higher consciousness. Initially, most walk-ins are not consciously aware that a soul exchange has taken place, which means he or she may deal with temporary disorientation as to why they suddenly feel so different. He or she may notice changes in lifestyles and preferences or feel compelled to change their names, life partners, or jobs. Many walk-ins detach from the natal soul's family. Therefore, a divorce is not uncommon with walk-ins. Gradually, the soul becomes accustomed to being in a physical body on an unfamiliar planet.

While I personally did not have recognition of what was occurring prior to and during my walk-in, there are many souls who are aware of the contract they have made as a walk-in and know when the transfer is about to take place. Because conscious walk-ins have contact with higher dimensions and bring in full or partial memory of their mission, they seem to have a less traumatic transfer and don't have a major shift in personality.

Merging with Your Oversoul

A lot of people who have done the work of spiritual purification are starting to blend the energy of their Earth soul with their higher selves, monads, and soul groups. When your soul's vibration rate increases to a certain level, you may experience a soul shift or soul exchange.

An event that began August 1, 2011 not only increased the pace of my ascension process, it also brought greater clarity to my walk-in event. This created a desire for me to expand the scope of this book to include help for all who are experiencing ascension symptoms or need help with settling the dust after a spiritually-transforming experience. I believe that if people are more aware of what is happening to them, the ascension process will be much less painful and the work of soul development will progress easier and more quickly.

To help you better understand this linking of souls, I'll give a brief background about my walk-in and subsequent soul progression.

For clarity purposes, I refer to the natal soul (born into this body) as Bon—a nickname my family gave me when I was young. I use the name LavendarRose to refer to the soul that I am now. Prior to 1999, LavendarRose served as a spirit guide to Bon. As I've said before, souls are multidimensional. We exist in other planes and realms of consciousness where there is peaceful cooperation among beings of light. Bon and I are possibly twin flames, but even if not, we have partnered to assist one another with soul development. We have an agreement to either be incarnated at the same time in close relationship with another, or for one to serve as a guide while the other is in body.

In December of 1999, a soul exchange occurred during which LavendarRose walked into the body of a 40-year-old female. Bon walked out of this body and took a position in its auric field to observe this life from a spiritual vantage point. My family did not understand the sudden and drastic changes in my life that occurred as a result, and they would not have understood if I had tried to explain my walk-in. Many already thought I was crazy and I didn't want to do anything to lend support to that notion! Besides, I had never heard of a walk-in; I just kept thinking to myself that I had died and come back.

In late 2005, I began to sense that another significant soul shift was about to occur. By then, I had researched and knew about the walk-in process. I had read of multiple walk-in experiences in a body during one lifetime, and at first, I thought this meant that another soul exchange was about to take place for me. Following my intuition, I went to my primary care doctor with very few symptoms to support my sense that my body had a serious illness. The second doctor I saw decided to do a colonoscopy—most likely just to appease my relentless insistence that something was not right. Surgery was scheduled immediately after discovering a large tumor and several polyps that were on the verge of becoming cancerous. It was during colon surgery that Bon left her position in my auric field to prepare for her next incarnation. I grieved for a month prior to the surgery that facilitated her exit; however, when I awoke in the recovery room, I felt angels and benevolent spirit guides all around me. I heard their comforting words and instruction about breathing deeply as I became conscious. My guides told me beforehand that the surgery was being used to facilitate a spiritual experience and that my body would in no way suffer harm. My surgeon originally told me I would in the hospital for three to five days. I went home within 24 hours after surgery with hardly any pain at all, much to the surprise of the entire staff and my family. I stayed in a state of bliss for about two months afterward.

Before LavendarRose walked in, there was a unique and heavenly fragrance that I (and no one else) smelled constantly. After my colon surgery, I no longer smelled the fragrance. This is what let me know that Bon had left completely. In 2009, Bon visited me in my dream to let me know she was incarnating as a member of my family. For three days after that dream I smelled the wonderful fragrance and was in a state of emotional bliss as I floated through life with ease. Then, the fragrance was gone as mysteriously as it had appeared.

While driving down Andrew Jackson Parkway on August 1, 2011 the fragrance came in so strong that I immediately inquired about what was going on. Was my newly incarnated twin soul in trouble? Why was this family member visiting me in spirit? (I am not at liberty to reveal the identity of this person, but I'll use LR2 as a pseudonym.) In response to my question, I heard, "I am not LR2; I am Bon." That confused me because I understood that Bon had reincarnated as LR2. The voice accompanying the fragrance spoke again, "After reaching purer levels of consciousness and achieving significant progress in soul development, the soul that you call Bon has expanded into two souls. LR2 is one part of the soul and I am the other part."

I am very happy with my life and my spiritual expression and do not want to experience another adjustment phase like the one I went through after the soul exchange in 1999. Concerned that another walk-in was about to occur, I wanted to prevent further abuse to this physical body. Souls can say no to walking out, even if it is in their contract. I refused another soul exchange, but needed clarity about what was happening. I felt like a different person—probably because I was spiritually and emotionally in a near-orgasmic state of being 24/7 for twelve days.

Overlighting

The soul or consciousness is a higher vibration of the personality that resides in the physical body. At least a dozen aspects or essences of the soul/oversoul/ higher self are in the area above our head at the crown chakra. This group is called a monad or soul group.

Overlighting is when an aspect of your soul or oversoul, ascended masters, spirit guides, teachers, or angels drape their energy over you for a period of time. During my twelve days of ecstatic bliss, I sought the counsel of Dr. Caron Goode to gather what information she might provide regarding this situation. I gave her as few details as possible so she would not be guided by my interpretation. Caron didn't sense that a walk-in was occurring. Instead, she saw an eighth- or ninth-dimensional being draping over my physical body. Only my feet and lower legs were showing. The artwork on the cover of this book is a representation of what she saw.

During an overlighting arrangement, a person is able to take advantage of the spiritual knowledge of the higher aspect of the oversoul; and the oversoul is able to anchor itself in the Earth plane through the physical body. Caron confirmed that a higher aspect of my soul was merging with this body to channel and assist the writing of this book. After twelve days of calmly merging this aspect of my oversoul with my physical body, the fragrance vanished. Mysteriously, this occurred within minutes after a visit with the family member (LR2), who carries one of the souls of Bon, which I now understand is a soul group.

I was troubled that the fragrance had left. Did this mean that my oversoul was not going to help me write this book? Did it mean my twin flame had left? My emotional bliss waned with these thoughts. I again consulted Dr. Goode. She heard, "Integration complete." The experience I had this time was not a soul exchange. During this overlighting, I had received a download of the purer energy from my soul group/monad. This merging is what some refer to as a soul braid.

I noted several changes once this merging was complete. Even though I had worked extensively on resolving karma left by the natal soul (Bon), some of the deeper emotional wounds of her childhood started coming to the surface to be healed. I began having an urge to fast one day per week as I had done regularly in the mid-1990s. The Yamaha keyboard that Bon used to play for hours each day came out of the closet where it had been stored for years. I used it to create music to go with verbal affirmations to assist with soul development. I added these MP3s to my Website: WeAre1inSpirit.com and some of them are offered as 99-cent downloads on Amazon.com.

Dissociation

My soul exchange in 1999 occurred during a dissociative state and I've learned that dissociation due to traumatic experiences is a common response to distress. I've asked my friend and colleague, Dr. Caron Goode, who provides wonderful support and encouragement to me on my spiritual journey, to share her insight. She is a nationally-certified counselor with membership in the American Psychotherapy Association. As a spiritually-advanced person who has successfully integrated the influx of purer vibrating energy she received during her walk-in experience in the 1990s, Caron brings much wisdom to this topic.

Caron notes that PSTD (post-traumatic stress disorder) is prevalent among those who have been in war zones, experienced physical or emotional abuse, or had a near-death experience or other intense upsetting situation. "When stressed, men and women tend to respond differently," says Caron. "Men tend to act out and show aggressiveness. Women tend to withdraw and dissociate. Dissociation can be mild like daydreaming, fantasizing, or losing time when driving, watching television, or absorbed in a good book. The more distress, trauma, or pain a person experiences, the more serious a dissociative response can be. Some have difficulties in identity, like feeling so detached that they view themselves as a robot. Other problems include lack of memory and over-sensitivity in feelings and empathy, all of which most walk-ins experience. This is why focusing on integration and recognizing the way energy works is so important. Understanding how the mind, emotions, and body work in conjunction with the soul's purpose makes integration easier and less stressful. It permits you to have more compassion for yourself while growing into the higher self.

"While people in other cultures sometimes have dissociative experiences in the course of religious (in certain trance states) or other group activities, these 'spiritual experiences' are finally becoming accepted in Western cultures. And while some walk-ins have entered through such an experience, the ability to identify with the body, feel emotions, and take charge of the integration process may not be easy. One of the issues facing individuals during the ascension process is the level of distress stored in the brain/body and the unknown compartmentalized memories that can pop up any time. Here's why.

"Recent studies of trauma indicate that the human brain stores traumatic memories in a different way than normal memories. Traumatic memories are not processed or integrated into a person's ongoing life in the same fashion as normal memories. Instead, they are dissociated, or "split off," and may erupt into consciousness from time to time without warning. The effected person cannot control or "edit" these memories. Over a period of time, these two sets of memories, the normal and the traumatic, may coexist as parallel sets without being combined or blended. These traumatic memories still need healing, and they can also pop up for the rest of the time you inhabit the body.

"Much healing and integration work can be done through energy transmissions and healings. However, the integration process is *so much easier* when the person can feel, read, and know what is happening on an energy level. What a clairvoyant may see as *done* or an energy healer pronounce as *healed* means nothing if the effected person is not cognizant of the process, and cannot translate those events into time and with personal meaning.

"A walk-in is here to take charge of the brain/body system, integrate the scattered soul fragments, and evolve into wholeness that will allow a mature expression of spirituality. To be fully empowered, enriched as a human being, and fulfilled in the work you came to do, the foundation is living and "being present" in the body. Spiritual teacher Ajaib Singh once said that living in the human body is the ultimate spiritual gift because the body is the direct polarity from the Spirit. It means that one can experience the richness of both at the same time.

"As you know, the brain/body/soul system is an exquisite energy array, dynamic, ever changing, and easily attuned, like a tuning fork. It is so easy to want to work only on an energetic level, and not be in time with your feet grounded. Yet, the conscious walk-in soul steps into the body already in a dissociative state. I propose the first place to integrate is not at the energetic level, but at the brain/body level. The whole key to the human brain/body is that energy has to move. That's it. Energy has to move.

"**Physical**: The first job is to stay in the body. An exercise program seems a necessity if we want to learn how to move, dance, walk, and experience the fullness and beauty of feeling human. Speaking and communicating with the endocrine system, your hormones, the gut, the heart, the colon, the shoulders that bear the burdens, and the feet that carry you through. All energy has consciousness and communicates in a personal way.

"**Emotions**: Don't be afraid of feelings, and do not indulge them either. When human emotions are the exquisite visceral feelings that tell us how we are doing and communicate the psyche's needs, we listen. When emotions are overpowering or we cannot control them, a simple rule of thumb is to do the following:

1. Be aware of them. Name them as energy in motion.
2. Listen, feel, or attune to the feeling in depth.
3. Get the message and acknowledge it; once they are thanked, feelings pass through.

4. If deep grieving and feelings seem immovable, then allow yourself the time to go fully into the richness of the experience, whether painful or traumatic, and move through the dark tunnel of emotional constriction until you feel the light of relief turn on inside, or you see the light and can move into it.

"**Intellect:** Think of all the intellectual information that the brain has acquired, being only as old as the physical body. Walk-ins who entered with awareness know that there are dimensions beyond the intellect where inspiration and silence resound. So the intellect does not ascend or go with the soul. Some fragmented life memories perhaps, but not the intellectual knowledge.

"The intellect has two primary jobs: to learn, to keep the body grounded, and to protect you from pain and fear. The intellect usually does this in the ways it has learned from role models. Typically, to keep the body grounded means to *do* something. Think of how when you are sick you cannot lie there and relax because the mind wants you to do something about the illness. How many times have you been ready for a breakthrough, and then sabotaged yourself or hit a wall and go, "Huh?" The intellect is doing its job. We thank the intellect for doing its role, and feed it as much inspiration as possible.

"Walk-ins and those who are ascending need the intellect to direct the daily activity and to keep them grounded. At the same time, you cannot rely on the intellect as your sole source of information. Higher guidance must come from your soul or your heart and is always your priority. Together, the soul and the brain can get you through and bring joy.

"The dissociation is like your consciousness alighting in the top of a tree, and your body sitting at the base of the tree on the ground. The distance between the two is the dissociated gap in consciousness, and your job is to close that gap by building bridges of character strengths.

• The intellect does well with praise

- The emotions do best with gratitude
- The body likes appreciation and care

"Always choose *to know.* The phrase, 'I do not know' cannot exist in your vocabulary! Your clear knowing is available to you 24/7 by focusing on your crown chakra and asking for guidance. Your integration includes being able to know your guidance and apply it in time. Sometimes there may be tension between your knowing something and wanting to act on it immediately. Your attunement to the knowing is first priority to be clear how things transpire in physical reality.

"Trusting your guidance comes with experience. Trust is a skill that the brain and body can learn as the energy system adapts and is comfortable with the walk-in as you become familiar with it. The more integrated you feel, the more trusting you are in your Earth walk."

Attempted Suicide

Any event that brings us face to face with death and the afterlife can cause a sudden shift in our consciousness. It's rarely business as usual for someone who attempts suicide. If the attempt resulted in the death of a loved one, the family is never the same again.

In exiting the Earth plane, the soul may leave by making the physical body ill and dying, or walking out during a soul transfer. I mentioned in my thoughts about immortality and wrote in my book, *More Than Meets the Eye ~ True Stories about Death, Dying, and Afterlife,* that there is always a choice about coming in and out of this 3-D world.

Many people have become emotionally distraught over the detrimental changes occurring on the planet and the suffering in their lives. Those who are in this type of physical and emotional pain want out of here—off the Earth. Without realizing it, a soul that is contemplating suicide is subconsciously offering its physical body to be inhabited by a new soul that is ready to incarnate. Even if a soul exchange was not agreed to prior to embodiment, the unsuccessful attempt at taking one's physical life can be the catalyst for a soul exchange.

Regardless of whether you walked in or were born in the body you now maintain, the soul you are now has a mission—not just to complete certain tasks in helping the Earth make this shift into fifth dimension, but to continue your personal evolution.

Starseeds

Do you ever sense that you are not from this planet or dimension? Even though it hasn't been proven, scientists have concluded that it is likely that there are other universes or dimensions where we are living and experiencing simultaneous, parallel lives. One part of our consciousness is in this third-dimension reality on Earth and another part of our consciousness is simultaneously living in higher dimensions. This might explain why many people are feeling scattered or having cases of deja' vu, or sensing past, present, and future moments simultaneously.

Starseeds are souls that have visited or lived on other planets or in other universes before incarnating on Earth. These universal travelers typically show up in human bodies *not* as the cartoon-like alien characters that travel in spaceships as Hollywood movies have depicted. That's not to say that these kinds of beings haven't lived on the planet before. We have structures on Earth like the Great Pyramids that even scientists say could not have been constructed without equipment or forces of supernatural levitation beyond what humans now possess. In light of the damage and destruction we have done to our own planet, it seems arrogant to think that we Earthlings have made it this far on our own. Still, most people have not accepted the notion that humans are *not* the only intelligent beings in our universe.

The Nephilim or "sons of God" mentioned in Genesis 6 were most likely part of the multitude of wicked beings cast out of heaven with Lucifer. My theory (although I cannot prove it) is that these aliens arrived from another dimension. They were genetically different than humans; they stood as tall as the cedar trees and possessed super-human strength. Numbers 13:32-33, states that the Hebrew spies reported seeing fearsome giants in Canaan. The account of David and the Philistine giant, Goliath, indicates that these super humans were still on the Earth after the Great Flood. These god-like beings married human women referred to as "daughters of man" and created a race of hybrid humans known as the Anakim. Mythology has the origin of these beings as from the constellation of Orion.

While none of us have direct memory or irrefutable proof of what has occurred on Earth for past millions of years, we do have scientific proof that other civilizations have come and gone. There's nothing to prove that Atlantis and Lemuria did not exist—there's the mystery of the Bermuda Triangle where many airplanes and boats have mysteriously disappear. Perhaps that is a portal to another dimension. And the people of the Mayan civilization? Where did they go? Perhaps they were extra-terrestrials who went back to the dimension from whence they came. You don't think ETs have been on or part of the Earth's evolution? Think again. The word extra-terrestrial was not likely in the vocabulary of the scribes who wrote about "angels" or "giants" or "sons of God" that mated with humans. Genesis 6:1-4 of the Bible records the occurrence of Nephilim thusly:

> *And it came to pass, when men began to multiply on the face of the earth, and daughters were born unto them, that the sons of God saw the daughters of men that they were fair; and they took them wives of all which they chose . . . There were giants in the Earth in those days; and also after that, when the sons of God came in unto the daughters of men, and they bare children to them, the same became mighty men which were of old, men of renown.*

If you were an ancient scribe, what would you have called a being that fell from the sky or arrived in a spaceship? Maybe you would have called them giants, or sons of the gods, or angels? What about an alien space craft that had "magical" power? Maybe you, like the Israelites, would have been afraid of it, and hidden it where no one would happen upon it incidentally. Perhaps you would have called it "The Ark of the Covenant."

As strange and unsettling as it may be for some people to consider, there is scientific evident that our current race of humans is not the only race which has inhabited planet Earth. We are not alone in this universe. We are more than global citizens; we are universal citizens, who are about to learn how to interact on a higher level of consciousness.

Chapter 4 ~ Signs of Ascension

The ascension or spiritual awakening is the shift we are all making on our path home to Source—oneness. We are leaving the condition of duality and separation where ego reigns over our thoughts, emotions, and actions.

Symptoms—the physical and emotional responses we have to this process—may come in the form of sickness, body aches and pains, financial loss, emotional despair, or an opening of supernatural abilities. Thankfully, the energy to heal the symptoms is also available. To share healing energy and reconnect you to the Sacred Heart is one of the purposes of this book. The Sacred Heart is the Garden of Eden where there is oneness with God and love for all of creation.

Healing is a journey that we all must walk on our way back to Source from whence we came and are still a part of. Therefore, disease, sickness, and illness are not signs of weakness; they can be signs that the body is moving toward becoming a multidimensional structure that can move beyond this 3-D carbon-based existence. Where one person sees an illness as a curse or failure, another person sees it as a learning device or cleansing tool that reminds us of our power to create whatever we want. There are many causes for illness. Perhaps something from a past life has blocked an energy center; perhaps it represents some wound in this lifetime residing in your cellular memory that is being brought to your attention so it can be healed.

Some of the symptoms we are now experiencing are related to the ascension process. We are working through karma; cleansing our minds, emotions, and bodies; and re-patterning our habits as we move forward on our path to oneness. Listening to our higher self, we are attempting to embody master presence in this physical body.

Connecting with the inner self and the Sacred Heart is a wonderful way to reduce ascension symptoms while finding a great amount of peace even though the world around us—even our own body—seems to be out of control. Disease or illness comes to us as a message. Listen to what your body and intuition have to say. Follow this intimate and uplifting instruction. Dr. Susan Allison has written a great book, *Empowered Healer*, which has an accompanying CD that can teach you exactly how to do this.

As you ascend, you may have noticed that your likes and dislikes are changing. Situations and even people that you once enjoyed no longer appeal to you. You are giving up habits that you thought impossible to let go of. Material possessions may not mean as much to you as they once did. You may have the "urge to purge" and get rid of belongings and clean out closets (both physical and emotional ones). You have a keen sensitivity to the energy around you—you may even feel what animals, plants, and insects feel. You may feel loving and at one with everything. I cried one day because I accidentally killed a wasp! I truly was not expecting that response. Some things you were once involved in—even your job—may now seem unfavorable, and you either have made a career change or are thinking of trying something new. You may have a tremendous urge to give up substances or get help with an addiction. You may be seeking counseling for a troubled relationship, or you may have decided that it's time to let go of a relationship and move on without a significant other.

Ascension anchors and embraces another level of spiritual awareness. I'm hearing more and more people admit that they are able to see, hear, and sense non-physical spirits around them. The children coming in to the Earth plane now seem to have this ability and they are bringing in skills they learned in past lives. All of these "symptoms" can be signs of spiritual growth.

The shift naturally requires change and that's the very thing many humans are most afraid of. Some changes are great and you can see the benefit very quickly; other situations may seem troublesome as you walk through them. It may seem as though you are being pushed beyond your comfort zone as multiple areas of your life shift at once, but the universe is always supporting you even when things feel chaotic. It's important to trust that these changes are blessings in disguise. By yielding to these changes rather than resisting them, we find peace even in the uncertainty we may feel as we embark on a new path. We might as well relax and enjoy the ride because it is taking us to a better place. My interview with Vickie B. Majors, the artist who created the cover art for this book, talks about accepting change as we transition. You can hear that podcast for free at http://dld.bz/aC4Cx.

Spiritual awakening means no longer seeing yourself as a victim or a separate being. It refers to a growing awareness of the reality of our oneness with our creator and each other. It means life, lived to the fullest moment by moment. This awakening will be different for each person because as individuations of the divine we each have unique personalities and life experiences. Awakening can manifest in an instant like a flash of lightning or we may move through periods of spiritual growth spurts—we may even have phases when it feels like we are going backward or it seems like we are being tested to see how much we have learned. Over the years the changes we are making become noticeable and permanent.

Examples of Oneness through Technology

Through the ascension process we are leaving behind the idea that we are separate from our creator and one another. You've probably noticed how easily children pick up on using the Internet, cell phones, video games, cameras, and other technological devices. My cousin's four-year-old grandson performed an unsupervised Google search and then called his parents to the computer to see the Wii Fitness Plus game he wanted them to buy him. This ability to intuitively focus on what we want to manifest is a forerunner of the telepathic skills that I believe we will soon be using.

The computer and the Internet are examples of our oneness. We have a wealth of information and divine intelligence inside of us, even though we may not use all of it. Turn on the computer (or other devices such as a smart phone or wireless tablet) and you can access a portal of information known as the Internet. Although no one knows "where" the Web resides, it is interconnected with strands of information linking to sites everywhere—multi-dimensionally perhaps. We can find historical facts and photos about any event. This can cause us to feel as though we were physically there to experience it when it was occurring.

This ability correlates to our past lives. Humans are able to read one another's pages (mind, energy) to ascertain information about them—hopefully to better understand or help them. The Internet parallels this ability by connecting us on social networking sites. We awake each day to new posts on our Facebook wall or Twitter stream. People reveal a lot about themselves on these sites, which gives us a sense of oneness and community as we navigate Earth life. We continue to socialize with them through our thoughts even when we are not connected to the Internet.

Our history is stored in the Akashic records, our genes, DNA, and cellular memory. We have etheric cords to everything we have experienced, everywhere we have been, and everyone we have met. This is paralleled as the browsing history and cache and "cookies" on our computers. Our steps can be traced back to the sites where we have left personal information and an energetic imprint.

Doing an energetic clearing on the body, chakras, or aura (electromagnetic field) is like cleaning the cache on your computer.

You can release psychic cords that connect you to the detrimental energy of other people. Because we are one, we can never completely disconnect from another person or anything that has happened. Therefore, *integrating* rather than *severing* the tie is a better choice. Integration is what the clearing exercises in this book will accomplish. You don't need to be protected from anything or anyone. You will find that integrating and transmuting (changing the vibration of the energy) is better than trying to get rid of it. Energy can't be destroyed; it can only be converted or transmuted into something else. Why not use all kinds of energy to bless your life and others?

Signs Indicating a Spiritual Awakening

Achieving a higher level of consciousness isn't accomplished by wishful thinking; it requires commitment, diligence, and sacrifice. Yet, the rewards far outweigh the discomfort. There have been times when I questioned my sanity as I walked this path, feeling very alone. I've had to confront my fears at every turn—I spent many a night in the early 1990s lying on the bathroom floor, physically sick from emotional despair. There were times when I fought to repress my intuition as this internal guidance tried to lead me into truth that my mind could not accept and that my church would not approve. I lost many friends who began to think of me as too far removed from the traditional teachings of the Christian faith in which I was raised. Without information or a guidebook or guru, it took me years to realize that physical and emotional pain comes from resisting the ascension process. There was no one to tell me how to regain my emotional health so I could keep going forward.

There's no need for anyone to go through such torment. As we enter these intense years of the shift into purer consciousness, there are spiritually-minded folks all over the world willing and able to help. A Google or Facebook search will help you find a group where you can chat and find community.

Having said that, I will give a few signs, which indicate that we as individuals and a collective society are going through a spiritual awakening. While writing this chapter on symptoms, it seems that the universe wanted me to experience as many as possible! I've had most of them. This list is by no means complete, but these are a few of the more common symptoms that people have reported in regards to spiritual growth. Some of these are from this excellent video: http://youtu.be/txTsbeuY5gM.

Anxiety or Panic Attacks

As things change within the body, it affects the emotions and vice versa. Most people fear unsolicited change and may resist the Spirit's attempt to rid the mind of fear-based patterns of thinking. This can manifest as anxiety, nervousness, or panic attacks.

Anxiety is a sign that you are resisting a clearing process. Simply acknowledge this emotion that has come up for healing. This fragmented part of your soul is asking to be integrated and aligned with the purer vibration of your soul. Breathe and bring it into the flow of life—anxiety is just another form of energy. When you feel nervous, remind yourself that this is only energy moving through. Say something like: "I allow dense/dark energy to be transmuted and integrated into love/light energy as I enjoy my peaceful, prosperous, easy life."

Use the tools you have discovered and keep repeating the mantras, prayers, and affirmations listed in Chapter 5 of this book. By the time you memorize them they will have started shifting your response mechanism and you will begin to address anxiety in a new way.

Panic attacks can be "talked down" by tapping into the Sacred Heart center (see Chapter 5). Reading a passage in *A Course in Miracles* gets my mind calmed down and into better perspective rather quickly. Certain herbs have been found useful for treating nervousness. Talk with an herbalist or alternative health practitioner about using valerian root, passion flower, kava kava, St. John's wort, or other herbal supplements.

Sometimes the intense energy one feels as anxiety is actually a buildup of faster-vibrating frequencies that need to be released. The best way to do this is to get into the Sacred Heart space for five minutes. Do some deep breathing (see chapter 5) and then envision a ray of light beaming from your heart center toward anyone you feel needs a boost of God-Goddess love and light. If you don't have a particular person in mind, send that beam into the collective consciousness of humanity.

Body Sensations

As the biological body shifts into the light body, the old cellular structure is dissolving, giving birth to a new crystalline structure. For some who are sensitive, this can be an uncomfortable experience until enough of the form has been transmuted to allow for a purer vibration to take hold. The detoxification process can bring about body aches and pains (flu-like symptoms) or fatigue that our current medical doctors cannot explain or treat. It is not uncommon to experience unusual sensations in your body or chakras. There could be pressure on top of your head, tingling on your scalp or forehead (especially between your eyebrows), or energy surges in your body. Pain, hot flashes, and chills are also reported.

Body aches and pains may be directly related to regions in the subtle bodies that are blocked or stuck. Headaches may indicate that the third eye is opening. Stomachaches could indicate that you are stuffing your feelings/emotions. Chronic cough and sore throat may indicate a blocked fifth chakra. These symptoms should subside once the energetic condition is cleared and the body has acclimated to the new vibration. Until then, take advantage of energy therapy, acupuncture, aromatherapy, exercise, herbs, homeopathic remedies, mineral and vitamin supplements, salt baths, massage, or other holistic methods necessary to handle the discomfort.

Because organs and glands within the body are changing to accommodate the light body, your arms, hands, feet, or legs may tingle when you are meditating or doing conscious breathing. For more than ten years, I have experienced the sensation that someone is lightly touching or playing with my hair. I've also felt that I'm half in and half out of my body or that my spirit is too large to fit inside my skin.

Change of Relationships & Careers

Karma is what keeps us stuck in certain patterns and relationships. As you transcend karma, it naturally brings about change within your life. It's not uncommon to end a long-term relationship, or no longer associate with some family members as the astral body is cleared of soul contracts or etheric cords to people with whom there was karma to resolve. There's no need to feel bad if you need to separate yourself from people who try to dump their stuff on you and drag you into their problems.

You might also change careers or end a long-term employment. Many people are starting home-based businesses that are more aligned with their personal truth and life mission.

Creativity and Energy Surges

Have you noticed an increase in creativity? Perhaps you are more artistic, feeling more creative, or have a sudden interest in music or dance. I went crafting crazy during the 2011 holiday season! You might find that you are using seemingly new skills that you were not formally taught. A friend of mine recently told me that she was able to speak in what seemed like a language that she had not learned and did not understand. I had to laugh because my Pentecostal friends figured that one out a long time ago! Possibly, these "tongues" are languages that we spoke in previous lifetimes, or they may be languages of light and sound that only the soul or other-worldly beings understand. As time is speeding up, all lifetimes (past, present, and future) are being merged. This is part of the process of becoming whole.

Decluttering, Detoxing, and Simplifying

Sell, toss, and repurpose! Do you sense a need to detoxify, declutter, and simplify your life? You may be asking yourself "Why am I keeping this junk? I don't even remember why I wanted this item." My spending patterns have changed. I buy less quantity and higher quality. I have no reservation about purchasing something I need; yet, I have patience to wait until I find what I really want before I make a purchase.

I've been cleaning out and giving stuff away on a regular basis. I can feel the energy shift when I clean a room or closet. Not just my physical dwelling, but my computer files as well. I just can't stand clutter.

I've also been on a reduce-reuse-recycle campaign and admit that it feels good to donate stuff to charity, knowing that someone else may find it useful. I think Lynn Serafinn's book, *The 7 Graces of Marketing: how to heal humanity and the planet by changing the way we sell,* has had a profound influence on me. While I don't tend to store things needlessly, I can typically see a new purpose for an old item and I'm quick to adapt it.

You may also get the urge to detox your own body. I find myself asking, "Why do I want to eat/drink this unhealthy stuff?" If I can't answer with a reason that satisfies my spirit, I find something else to nourish my body.

Depression and Loss of Interest

You may experience a change in interests and aspirations or find that you are simply not interested in the people and things that you once were. As old issues come back, you may experience sudden waves of emotion such as crying, anger, loneliness, or sadness.

Depression is common when something is coming up for healing. It will pass as soon as it is processed.

It was commonplace each year for as long as I can remember for me to experience some seasonal depression due to the lack of sunlight and daylight hours in the winter. However, I was having one of the best winters ever in late 2011. For Christmas, my husband got one of those machines that converts LP vinyl albums and cassettes into MP3 files. In early January 2012, I was on a cleaning and reorganizing rampage and decided to go through a box of cassette tapes stored in the top of the den closet. There were about a hundred recorded hours of me playing the piano during the early 1980s to late 1990s when I was the church pianist and accompanist for soloists, quartets, trios, youth choirs, and church choirs. Converting the tapes into a digital format would preserve them, but it meant I had to listen to them in real-time. For several days, I laughed hysterically at the amateur lyrics of the songs I had written during the days when I aspired to be a famous songwriter. I found a tape of me interacting with my children when they were preschool age. I enjoyed hearing them sing their ABCs and recite nursery rhymes, and got a big kick out of my daughter's dismay at discovering that Humpty Dumpty was an egg. I re-experienced my Liberace renditions of "It is Well with My Soul," "Ivory Palaces," and "When I Survey the Wondrous Cross" from my Southern Baptist days. I went even farther down memory lane as I tripped over the shaped-notes of my southern gospel playing style from the old red-back *Church Hymnal* and *Inspiration No. 4* that we used in the church I attended as a child and teenager.

Even after the task was completed, I felt like "Traveling On" and found myself still sailing in "The Good Old Gospel Ship," envisioning my mansion over the hilltop, and "Winging My Way Back Home" while having a "Little Talk with Jesus." Then, suddenly it hit me. I became so depressed that I didn't want to get out of bed. My body ached, and I kept right on binging on chocolate, coffee, sodas, and other comfort foods. Overnight, I had lost all interest in my work, and refused to answer the phone because I didn't want to talk with anyone or be around people. I was an emotional mess, swinging from bouts of anger to episodes of crying for no apparent reason. Since I had felt so good for so long, this dejected condition really troubled me. If only I could meditate or exercise my body. But, those desires had left too. I knew it was related to some residual energy I was releasing regarding my church days, first marriage, and motherhood. Therefore, I decided not to resist it. I cried. I moped. I felt whatever it was that came up and I asked my guides to help me process whatever was going on.

I purchased a bottle of St. John's wort, a multi-vitamin, and vitamin D supplements. Before these remedies even had a chance to work, a friend called and wanted to get together on Friday. I really didn't want to be near anyone while I was in this funk, but my husband had admonished me to not let this energy consume me, so I agreed to do a "juicing" with her. When Vickie came over, her energy was so bright and loving it was contagious. As we fed the raw fruits and veggies into the juicer, I began feeling lighter, as if a cloud were lifting from me. In less than an hour after drinking this healthy concoction and being in her presence, I was really enjoying our time together and was glad I had agreed to this visit. By the time Vickie left, I was laughing, and all that depressive energy had been completely dispelled. It has not returned.

This says a lot—not only about ascension symptoms being real—but about how important it is to be around people whose vibration is pure. Because I was constantly doing ascension exercises and affirmations in an effort to raise my own vibration, it was easy to "match pitch" with Vickie's energy.

Desire for Freedom

During the ascension process, some people have an intense desire to break free of restrictive habits that no longer serve them. We are seeing this worldwide trend of awakening sweeping the planet via demonstrations to bring freedom from repressive governments. Occupy Wall Street began in New York and has spread to numerous cities, demanding change in the political and economic systems to provide equal sharing of all the world's resources. This and other movements indicate the desire to end the suffering of separatism and bring oneness and unity to all people.

Additionally, you may know that you are supposed to move to another area, state, or country regardless of whether you understand *where* you need to be. Do you have a strong desire or impulse to wander or travel and explore the world? I have a friend who has moved about once a year for the past five years. She's still restless. Sound familiar?

One way to find freedom from worry is to stop judging yourself and others. "Do not take the name of God in vain" is not a statement promoting the egotistical characteristics of a man-made deity ready to punish those who do not obey. Rather, it is a reminder that the almighty "I AM" presence of the God-force lives within each of us. Our words and feelings are powerful, yet most people don't realize that both blessing and cursing abide in the tongue (speech). When we harshly judge or punish ourselves, feel guilt or shame, or say things like "I'm not good enough," or "I'm so stupid," it activates the creative power of God (which always responds with "yes") and curses the very life force, vitality, health, and positive emotions within your body and auric field.

The same thing happens when you speak ill will toward others. Honoring the free will of another person is important if you want inner peace. When you cannot allow and honor the choices that other people make, you put yourself under the law of sin and death (karma) rather than living in the law of grace (freedom).

Dietary Preferences

As you take more control of your life and become more responsible for your thoughts, it is natural that you will also make changes to the choices you make regarding your food. A return to our connection with Mother Earth is leading many people to grow their own food and abstain from eating the flesh, eggs, and fluids of animals.

Americans have been brainwashed to think that they need animal protein in order to be healthy. Nothing could be farther from the truth. If only you knew of the unsanitary conditions in which animals are raised and packaged for consumption you might change your mind. Research done by Dr. Will Tuttle shows that animals pick up bacterial, fecal contamination, cancerous tumors, and other health problems on their way to the market. They are treated with antibiotics, which are given with unsterilized needles used on multiple animals. And the hormones they are given in factory farms get stored in the cells of the animal's bodies. When humans eat these animals, toxins, diseases, and uric acid are transferred and trapped in the fat cells in the human. How can this *not* have an effect upon the cells of our bodies? Herbivores are fed high-calorie animal products to fatten them up for slaughter. How have we failed to see this as having a connection with the obesity, diabetes, and heart problem in our country?

Plants, fruits, vegetables, legumes, and whole grains provide much better nutrition (including protein) than processed foods and animal flesh. And, in addition to not having the capacity to feel or form communities as mammals do, most plants actually are stimulated to reproduce by the "pruning" required to harvest them. For more information, I recommend Dr. Will Tuttle's book, *The World Peace Diet* (http://www.worldpeacediet.org).

You may find you are eating lesser quantity than usual; or you may eat more frequently or less often—even fasting or going on a detox/cleanse for the body. You may have cravings for foods that you normally do not desire. If you are craving salty foods and feel bloated with water retention, drink lots of water to flush the system and take nightly baths with Epsom salts to draw out excess sodium or potassium through the skin. If you are craving sugar and other comfort goods, you may be resisting the process of clearing the temple of the Holy Spirit.

You may have to rearrange your life in order to place your spiritual journey as a priority above other endeavors. For example, drinking alcohol, eating junk food, or depriving your body of sleep in order to maintain an active nightlife may not serve you during the ascension process. During the writing of this book, I became so sensitive to alcohol that I had to cut it completely out of my diet. I encourage you to follow your intuition and do whatever is necessary to maintain physical health while your body ascends.

Electronic Disturbances

You may have noticed some electrical disturbances with computers and other electronic devices. You may experience things like driving down the street when suddenly all the light bulbs flicker or turn on/off. After stopping about four watches dead in their tracks within a six-month period in the early 2000s, I stopped wearing a watch. If the universe wants me to know what time it is, there will be a clock within sight.

During meditation in my bedroom one day, I heard a loud vibrating noise in the adjoining bathroom. I jumped up to see what was going on and found my electric razor buzzing around in the wooden tray where I keep it! When we meditate, we raise the vibration of our own body and the surrounding area.

I've had musical toys in the den closet come on automatically. It was pretty freaky when Little Leap starting singing the ABC song when no one was in the room! These types of disturbances could also be caused by the increase in cosmic energy penetrating the Earth's atmosphere. However, being an empath who is able to sense subtle energy shifts, I felt an earthbound soul was responsible for that particular incident. Someone, whom I know has entities attached to his field, had just left my house five minutes before. I do not allow earthbound souls to stay in my home, so I let it know it could either find its host, who was only a few miles down the road, or go into the light. I lit a bundle of sage and the energy of the room immediately shifted back into a peaceful state. Sage-o-matic!

One empath I chatted with said she seemed to disable cellphones, wireless devices like printers, keyboards, etc. Her boss used to think she was purposely breaking them. Her printer fried twice for no apparent reason. After that, her boss accused her of being into witchcraft and started telling her how important religion was in society. Be careful not to retaliate if something like this happens. Our thoughts are energetic forms that have tremendous power. I'm cautious to send only loving thoughts and energy toward my computer and other electronic devices I own or use.

Fatigue

Your body is responding to accelerated frequencies by changing its DNA and physical functions/processes to include light as a fuel source. Therefore, if you are not getting enough sunlight, you may feel more aches and pains, especially in the mornings. I have found that more sunlight and a supplement of vitamin D3 helps—particularly in winter.

As the body moves into faster vibration, it requires more energy, which means your normal six to eight hours of sleep may not be enough—especially if you are dealing with health issues. I find that yoga stretches and other forms of body movement help me feel more energized because these actions collect chi and direct it throughout the body. If you tire easily or experience fatigue throughout the day, your body may be urging you to rest, sleep, exercise, stretch, and eat/drink more healthily. Give your body what it needs, which may include nine to twelve hours of sleep in each 24-hour period.

You've no doubt heard of chronic fatigue syndrome and fibromyalgia. While this can come as a result of taking on the energy of someone else in order to transmute it, some of the aches, pains, and lethargy we feel as we age are from years of toxins building up in the body. Antibiotics and an acidic diet (high in sugar, alcohol, animal products, and processed foods) can create an internal environment for yeast to grow to a toxic level. Left untreated or given improper treatment, this condition can invite cancer cells to grow or put one at risk of diabetes and heart problems. I'm stating this because many people have yeast overpopulation in their bodies and don't realize what is causing them to feel so bad—they may even think they are just having ascension symptoms. In one way, all this *is* ascension related because this shift we are making is pushing every detrimental thing to the light and giving us a chance to cleanse it, modify our lifestyle, and transfer into our light body. Never brush off your body's signals or your intuitive clues as unimportant. If you sense that there is an underlying medical problem, please see your holistic medical doctor for treatment.

Headaches

I've read in several sources that an increase in the size of the pituitary gland or pineal gland (associated with the third eye) may be causing unexplained headaches for some. The bud of the pituitary has 1,000 separate petals, also known as the 1,000-petal lotus as described by Buddha. Each bud in the pituitary produces a different chemical necessary to bring forth biological ascension. On page 100 of *What is Lightbody?* Tashira Tachi-ren gives an exercise in which you use your hands and visualization to pull the cranial plates apart. A cranial-sacral practitioner may also be of use for reducing headaches associated with the ascension process.

Heart Palpitations

The ascension process can cause physical, emotional, and mental overload. Some people report heart palpitations with difficulty breathing and have thought they were having a heart attack. Two close family members who are on a path to ascension have been having irregular heartbeats and/or a racing pulse. Both had EKGs that showed their hearts are fine. When nothing abnormal can be found in medical testing for heart health, these symptoms may be attributed to the opening of the heart chakra.

As with headaches and other discomforts mention here, never take for granted that what you are experiencing is just an ascension symptom. Listen to your body's wisdom and get the help you need.

Hot Flashes or Kundalini Rising

Kundalini is hot energy, like fire, and allows for the burning off of karma, contracts, and soul agreements that must be released in order to ascend. The Kundalini has often been associated with sexuality, but sexual activity is not necessary in order for the Kundalini to awaken. During these hot flashes and sudden sweats (both day and night), the toxins that are being released in the biological transmutation process are being pushed out through the pores of the skin.

This hot energy that hits suddenly is so intense at times that you may feel a slight state of panic as it surges through your body. It used to be that only women going through menopause experienced hot flashes. These days, young women and even *men* are having hot flashes and are sensing the rising of a faster vibrating Kundalini energy system. I had "tropical meltdowns" for three years before I finally went to a holistic doctor who was able to treat me with natural supplements and bio-identical hormones, which helped greatly.

And, it's not just hot flashes! Many are reporting cold flashes as well. These conditions are not dependent upon the temperature in the room. They come instantly and randomly.

Increased Emotional Responses

Emotional issues you thought were healed may be reappearing. It is common for old emotional patterns to resurface to be cleansed and healed at deeper levels. You may notice your limiting beliefs and self-destructive patterns emerging. You may have flashbacks of repressed memories stored at the cellular level. Acknowledge these emotions, but stay present and non-resistant. Simply allow them to flow through. On the other side of this coin, you may have fewer emotional responses to what is going on around you. Things that used to bother you don't even register on your "who gives a crap" meter.

Many people in the online groups that I participate in (such as the Empathy Connection on Facebook) are noting an increase in their emotional responses to the pain and suffering of others. They pick up on the thoughts, feelings, emotions, or even physical illnesses around them and may feel sadness, anger, panic attacks, or anxiety that does not belong to them.

Intuition and Psychic Gifts Increased

Your intuition may be stronger than ever. You may have a direct knowing of something, a sense when something is right, or if someone is lying to you. You may get "goose bumps" or shivers through your body indicating the truth of something you are exposed to. Perhaps you see, sense, or hear spirit beings around you.

You may be more aware of subtler energies and be emotionally sensitive to the energy of others as your psychic awareness opens up. You may be able to feel what others are feeling or know what someone is thinking. You may hear your name being called or you may hear voices that others do not hear. I can't hear it well enough to decipher what is being said, but there are times when I can hear distant voices like the broadcast of a radio talk show.

Your five natural senses are becoming more sensitive as they tap into higher dimensions of energy. You may smell things that others don't. I mentioned the heavenly aroma that I associate with my natal soul. During my intercessory prayer days, I smelled a lot of supernatural fragrances such as lilacs or roses as well as sulphur and foul odors when praying for people.

Some people report having a sudden "spiritual awakening," accompanied with the feeling of clarity and empowerment. I felt this kind of shift right after the merging of my oversoul in August 2011.

Miraculous Healing

Miracles happen every day and they should increase as we ascend. Perhaps you have had a miraculous healing such as mine: I did several exercises to raise my vibration right before bed one night. I knew I had processed and cleared during my sleep when I awoke with a headache the next morning. I had read about different types of headaches and what the location of the pain indicated as far as ascension symptoms. The pain was in the middle of my forehead and between my eyes. I opened the book, *What is Lightbody?* and read that pressure between the eyebrows is an indication that the pineal gland is growing. I pressed the area with my fingers and felt some relief. This let me know I was indeed dealing with ascension symptoms and not sinus problems or any other physical malady.

Still not ruling out a physical reason for my headache, I ate breakfast and drank a glass of water that had been blessed with an invocation. I did an oracle card reading and got instruction to be near a body of water. I had planned to take a walk by the river; I even put on my walking shoes, but then postponed it because I just didn't have the energy to exercise in the heat that was already reaching into the '90s at 10 a.m. So, I went to the living room and lit a candle and some incense. I sat in the recliner to rest and listen for instruction about what I needed to do next.

I had done about twenty-five full-wave breaths (see Chapter 5) and was feeling a relaxing buzz when the phone next to me rang. It was my daughter dialing for my two-year-old grandson, who had found a photo of me and was calling my name when he came to her and grabbed her cell phone. He really didn't want to talk; he was following his guidance to connect with me for spiritual purposes. When I hung up the phone two minutes later, my headache was completely gone and my strength was restored.

Levitation

When you ascend, your body's frequencies speed up so much that you step into a lighter dimension—a higher frequency realm than the material world. You may feel lighter and actually experience your body rising from the earth. You may feel one with everything and have no sense of time or space while in this condition.

Libido

As the ascension process occurs, you may note a change in your libido. Overall, I think the urge to gratify sexual desires through pornography, illicit encounters, and sex without love decreases as one ascends. In its place there is fulfillment through intimacy and heartfelt joy as well as multiple and total body orgasms that can last for hours. Jealousy toward your partner is replaced with deep trust. When you join with another in sexual intimacy, you share the fullness of your own self-love and divinity, and there's no need to look outside of yourself for fulfillment. Because you truly become one with your partner as your energy fields merge during pleasurable intimate encounters, you communicate telepathically, which allows you to better understand and meet one another's needs.

Sexual energy is a very powerful and sacred fuel that can propel the soul into purer realms of consciousness. I believe one of the reasons sex has been so perverted today and deemed taboo by many religions is because of the divine power it contains. Most people are afraid of their own divinity. Society and religion have separated people from their sexuality and made them feel that it is shameful or dirty. Not only has this left them with emotional trauma, it has also cut them off from an infinite source of power, creativity, and expression. Ancient Goddess-worshipping cultures respected and understood the correct use of sexual energy and incorporated it into their rituals. Yogic disciplines and tantric arts teach how to channel life force and sexual energy within the body.

Tantric sex can assist in transforming the energy body, which in turn raises the vibration of the physical body. This raise in vibration moves the body toward becoming healthy as it cleanses organs, glands, and the central nervous system. Sexual energy can be circulated throughout the body, strengthening the physical and subtle bodies and clearing emotional issues. For more information about how to use sexual energy for ascension, see http://www.tantricsecrets.com.

Mental Thoughts

Because repressed issues from our shadow side are emerging to be healed and integrated, you may process some terribly negative thoughts (judgment, criticism) or see horrific mental scenes. You may think these internal visions are premonitions of something bad about to happen to you or someone you love. While you may get forewarnings that require you to take precaution, more than likely these thoughts and images are deeply-hidden fears buried in your psyche that are coming up to be integrated. I compare these "prods and pokes" to the proverbial "devil on your shoulder," urging you to engage in egotistical behavior. You always have the choice as to whether you will entertain them or integrate them.

Recently, I had a battle raging in my mind. The thoughts were so hateful that I felt embarrassed about what I was hearing. I knew that any resistance I put up would only cause me to attract more thoughts like this as well as things, people, energy, and situations I didn't want. Thus, I spent time in nature, did some deep breathing, and got some physical exercise to help move energy through more quickly. I focused on the "now" moment to remind myself that there are no problems that the love within me can't handle. I repeated mantras such as these: "In this now moment, I have peace of mind. In this place of heart-centered love, I am calm and at ease. There is nothing to fear or stew over in this now moment." I've included this mantra as an exercise in Chapter 5. I also created an MP3 of the mantras I used and am happy to share it with you. See the Audios tab on my Website, WeAre1nSpirit.com. The soothing background music will help to bring you into a state of heart-centered awareness and assist your efforts in moving past the ceiling that the ego has erected.

> For when you have aligned your heart in the foundation of the love of the Creator and you have aligned your will through your heart, then you shall find peace, strength, power. . . and the absolute.
>
> ~ Chief Standing Elk, Starknowledge TV

I continued to focus my awareness within my heart center and ask for light and love to expand from within me. Each time I had a thought that was out of alignment with the Love that I am, rather than having an absurd dialog with my ego, I drew my awareness back to a place of peace within and sought strength in the Sacred Heart (Christ Consciousness). Breakthrough came suddenly and powerfully. The negative thoughts vanished immediately and the peace that I had connected with in my heart center manifested in my daily experience.

I don't always have the time to do a formal meditation, so my guides and I agreed upon a simple phrase that I can think or speak whenever thoughts come up that are not aligned with love. Thoughts are energy and can be converted, but not destroyed. "Transmute and integrate" or "purer thoughts now!" represent my willingness to have these thoughts transmuted into kind, peaceful thoughts that are then integrated with the purer frequencies in my mental field. I encourage you to try this or your own phrase the next time you are disturbed by negative energy fragments.

I love what Susann Taylor Shier teaches in her book, *Soul Reunion*, about integrating this fragmented part of ourselves. She refers to these incongruent aspects of self as "inner land mines." She says that they are not enemies to be fought; instead, they are fear-based factors that we have created and buried in our subconscious at some point in our journey of separateness. Many times these self-sabotaging mechanisms crop up when we elect to move forward in the ascension process. Why? Because they want to come home to the Sacred Love within us and be part of the oneness we are experiencing. We can choose to no longer allow them to keep us in bondage; however, these fragmented parts of us cannot be removed, released, ignored, or done away with. They are emotional energy and must be converted into a different type of energy (at a purer frequency) or integrated into our human experience through practicing non-resistance. By bringing these wayward parts into the Sacred Heart, we give them a new role: to assist us in accessing even more Sacred Love within and making our personal energy field even stronger and brighter!

Ringing in the Ears (auditory sensations)

For as long as I can remember, I have heard a very high-frequency and very loud humming tone in my ears. It is never accompanied by pain or a feeling of being filled with fluid and I rarely ever experience dizziness. I thought everyone had this ringing until I was in my twenties and mentioned it to my doctor one day. He brushed it off as tinnitus. I knew intuitively that it was related to something spiritual because the spirit gives us messages in our body, mind, emotions, and physical senses.

Abraham, through Esther Hicks, says that this ringing is caused by resisting the guidance that is coming to you from higher planes of consciousness. It indicates that the body is not vibrating high enough to hear the message coming from accelerated vibration. It is a distortion or vibrational interruption as you reach for a vibration you are not up to speed with. The answer is to increase the body's vibration. While that may be an acceptable answer, I still maintain the intuitive hunch that this humming is a frequency attuned to a higher realm.

Synchronicities

Synchronicity is the experience of two or more events that seem unrelated or unlikely to occur together by chance and that are observed to occur together in a meaningful manner.

Have you noticed that the time between thinking something and seeing it manifested is far less than it once was? Are you realizing that when your emotions and feelings are alighted with your thoughts that your desires (and fears) come into play much more quickly? Do you ever feel like you've known someone even though you just met them? These are benchmarks of spiritual awakening and ascending into purer consciousness.

Things we never noticed or paid attention to before are being brought to our awareness. You may see symbols such as numbers on a digital clock or car tags, animals that reappear in your path, synchronicities (meaningful coincidences or events occurring in perfect timing), or other signs. The week of 11/11/11, I was parked in front of a fruit stand at a convenience store while my husband went in to make a purchase. When I looked up I noticed the number 11 that was printed on the boxes. I counted more than five number elevens. Five years ago, I would have walked by without even seeing this. These signs can reflect or mirror something going on within your psyche; they can be messages from your spiritual guidance team.

You may think about an old friend you haven't seen in years and within days (hours or minutes) she shows up or calls you. This happened to me in January. A woman I was close friends with in the 1980s and hadn't seen in two decades was on my mind for several days one week. I thought of how I would love to hear from her and know how she was doing. Spirit was tugging on both of our hearts. I was aware that she was tapping into my energy field, as I was hers. The next week, Linda found me on Facebook and emailed to catch up. These kinds of synchronicities have become so common I'm no longer surprised when they happen. I now expect them.

Sleep Patterns Changed (Insomnia)

This transitional time can be emotionally, mentally, and physically intense. You may find that you have restlessness, sleeplessness, and more dreams; or you may dream more vividly and remember your dreams. When you are processing a lot of emotions, the body may need time to recover.

You may sleep more or fewer hours than usual. I've noticed that my sleep patterns have changed. Some nights I sleep for ten hours without waking once. Other nights I may sleep for three hours and then lie awake for hours. I have started my day at 4:30 a.m. because my body felt rested and refused to sleep. Strangely, I feel great the days following these sleepless nights—especially if I listen to the MP3s I purchased that have silent subliminal messages and binaural beats designed to sync the right and left hemispheres of the brain (see Chapter 5).

Don't be surprised if you need to take naps or sleep at different times of the day. During my week of depression last January, I was so tired that I slept several hours one afternoon. That was very unusual for me; my most active and productive hours are typically after lunch. I encourage you to take it easy on yourself and pay attention to your physical needs.

Vision and Perception

Your eyesight may have changed and now you see colors you've never seen before. Your internal vision reveals images of things that are about to happen.

Your physical vision may be hazy or out of focus, causing you to think you need a new vision prescription. I've tried four pairs of new glasses, only to find that I see no better with the new prescription than I did with the old one. In fact, some days an old pair works better than the new one! I have three pairs of glasses on my desk and I may swap them out several times a day.

As you begin to have multidimensional sight, you may see objects that other people do not see, such as sparkles of light, shadows, orbs or balls of energy, grids of light, or movement from corner of your eyes. Objects may seem to shimmer, move, or fade. In the Bible, Paul was blinded on the Road to Damascus as a result of seeing Jesus in His light body. Our human eyes need to shift in order to see into brighter realms.

Do you find that you are no longer afraid of trying new ventures? Your perception of life is shifting and you may see a situation differently as if with new eyes, or your whole attitude toward something you once held as invincible truth has changed. Instead of judging others, you feel compassionate toward them, viewing them and their situation more kindly. Things that used to bother you just don't seem to matter as much. This may be because we are resolving our own karma, or that the karmic pattern we held with that person has been transmuted.

Youthfulness

Perhaps you feel younger or more childlike, or your friends say you look younger. When enough of the old, fear-based patterning is removed from your cells, you will look and feel younger. I enjoy playing on the floor with my grandkids, many times feeling and interacting as if I am their age. My body may be sore the next day, but my soul knows no age! I'm sure my body will catch up soon.

Chapter 5 ~ Tips for Integration and Wholeness

Love is the greatest power there is. I don't know of anyone who would not welcome the presence of unconditional love into their human experience. Yet, many people avoid the very activities that would bring more love into their hearts. It is natural to commune with whatever we love or hold valuable. If you love watching movies, you may own a huge library of DVDs; if you love walking in nature, you may take hiking trips; if you love cooking, you may often be in the kitchen trying new recipes. In other words, you will arrange your schedule to spend time engaging in an activity that you feel drawn to.

Material things or even people cannot bring us the level of joy, love, fulfillment, and satisfaction that spending time in the presence of your higher self (Holy Spirit) and your loving master teachers. When you feel a longing inside, what you really want is to experience more love.

This chapter will give tips for connecting to the Sacred Heart within, where we experience being nourished by its infinite resources. These exercises are designed to put you into position to access the oneness you already have in God-Goddess.

I will also give methods that support the body as it changes during the ascension process. This will be especially useful to those of you who are dealing with sudden changes resulting from an experience that catapulted you into a spiritual transformation. These tips will work for anyone trying to acclimate to the faster or lighter (less dense) vibrations coming from the central sun, planetary shifts, and galactic alignment of the Earth, or from your oversoul, soul group, or multidimensional aspects of self.

You've probably heard it said that we only use about 10 percent of our brain—and that's the most highly-evolved savant or educated person. So what about this 90 percent that is dormant? I believe it is being called into action as we enter purer planes of consciousness. Unlike in our third-dimensional world, these dimensions have less density. And, rather than experiencing physical and mental limitations like we do in human bodies here on this plane, the light body is able to travel inter-dimensionally and is able to access cosmic knowledge.

We also have sixty-four codes of amino acids, but our current DNA is only using twenty of them. Because ascension speeds things up and anchors other levels of awareness, I believe that the accelerated frequencies now available to us are changing our DNA. This naturally brings about a restoration of whatever has become diseased in the physical body. We can aid in this restoration process in numerous ways. I've listed several exercises and affirmations that are working for me, and I know there are plenty more that can be implemented.

The list below is an eclectic mix that includes a variety of traditions and esoteric practices. There are many others not included here that can be used as a spiritual purification tool to help the body ascend.

- Affirmations
- Baths and salt scrubs
- Being non-resistant
- Brainwave entrainment
- Conscious breathing
- Crystals and gem stones
- Dietary changes
- Embracing divine feminine energy

- Energy work
- Exercise
- Grounding and centering
- Heart-centering and activatlon
- Intention
- Mantras
- Meditation
- Offering forgiveness and refraining from judgment
- Prayer
- Rituals
- Sacred geometry
- Singing and intoning sounds
- Singing bowls
- Smudging
- Sunlight
- Visualization
- Walking in nature and communing with elementals
- Yoga

Let's look at some of these individually.

Affirmations

We create our reality with our thoughts. We have a choice about what we think about, but it can be difficult to switch gears when you are caught in a whirlwind of negativity. You can reprogram your mind with mantras, affirmations, and other tools mentioned in this chapter. Your spiritual practice of realigning your mind and thoughts must become a priority if you want to feel more peaceful and powerful.

I personally believe that Jesus used affirmations to remind Himself of a higher truth. Certain phrases that have been attributed to Jesus were not only part of His teaching, they were spoken whenever He was confronted by religious leaders. When He said things like "Satan, get thee behind me," He was reminding his ego that the higher mind of God/Goddess was in control. When He said

"I am the way, the truth, and the life," He was reminding His followers (and anyone who has a willingness to hear) that the way to our Creator was through the oneness He was demonstrating with his life.

I have successfully used affirmations for many years. This positive reprogramming of the mind replaces a negative thought with a positive thought and shifts your focus from what you *don't* want to what you *do* want. Even if you don't believe the affirmation at first, it is still beneficial because it makes suggestions to the subconscious mind and sends a message to the universe that you desire to create a change. Eventually, the affirmation will be your new belief and this reprogramming will begin to manifest as positive changes in all areas of your life.

Earlier in this book I noted that soon after the merging of my oversoul last August my musical talent desired to be expressed again. I was a former church pianist, but laid down that talent when my walk-in occurred. One way this energy is being expressed now is through the creation of MP3 audios that offer affirmations and meditations set to music that I created on my keyboard. Some of these are available for free (some cost 99¢) on my Website, http://weare1inspirit.com/spiritual-audios.htm. I'll include in this chapter the words to some of the affirmations that can help to calm your body, mind, and emotions and help integrate accelerated frequencies.

Daily Affirmations

Covering most aspects of life in general, this affirmation for daily use is free on my Website. Click the "Audios" tab to listen to the spoken words set to beautiful background music by Shirley Cason (used by permission).

I am honored and respected by all.

I am always safe and divinely protected.

Everything I need comes to me in perfect timing.

Everything I need to know is revealed to me.

I am loving and loved.

I am vibrantly healthy. I glow with the presence of my higher self.

I prosper wherever I turn. I have more than enough to meet my needs and bless others.

I am willing to change, grow, evolve, and ascend in order to accomplish my divine purpose.

I am a blessing to others and others bless me.

All is well in my world.

I am abundantly blessed and happy as I express the beauty and creativity of my heart.

I deserve the best in all areas of my life.

I am open to receive all good from the universe.

I clearly communicate my needs and take the time necessary to appreciate my body, know my true self, and grow spiritually.

I attract only kind and gentle life lessons and relationships into my life.

I understand the divine plan for my life. I have passion and energy to fulfill it with joy!

Affirmation: In this Now Moment

The reason many people are feeling so out of sync is because they are being asked to let go of anything that no longer serves their soul's higher purpose. They are clearing the detrimental energy left behind from many former lifetimes. Walk-ins also have to clear the residual energy of the natal soul that inhabited the body. This can manifest as anxiety or nervousness.

You can make it through this shift if you keep talking to yourself positively. The body obeys the mind, but the body has obeyed for many years the signal contained in underlying fear-based beliefs. Changing this old mindset and giving the body time to make the adjustment to your new belief is like turning a huge ship around. See your goal and stay your course. You will get there!

Whenever our physical body has a challenging situation, it is best to pull back and tend to it rather than continuing to push forward in helping others. Refresh, restore, heal, and then when you are able, you will have the energy, resources, and guidance needed to help others without harming yourself. One way to do this is by taking a few moments to breathe and listen to affirmations that support your new goal and remind you of where you want to be.

Next, is a meditation designed to help you focus on being fully present in the moment rather than living in the past or worrying about the future. It also helps bring peace and awareness of your multidimensional selves and connects your soul with your oversoul while you sleep.

As I end my day, I recount with gratitude all that has transpired. I have followed my inner guidance in everything that I have created. I am satisfied, and yet I yearn to continue to be a blessing and to be blessed in even greater ways.

As I enter this time of body rest tonight I bring with me all the experiences of this day and offer them for review as my soul in this Earth body connects with my soul group, spiritual council, and all my realities in multiple dimensions.

I recognize that I am here on this planet at this time with a divine mission to share love and teach others how to find peace within. I do this by setting an example of love, exuding gratitude, and having a peaceful existence.

I am at one with all my multidimensional selves. I am at one with my oversoul.

I am merging all my consciousness into one unified field of light so that my purpose of love, gratitude, and peace can more easily affect the aura of Mother Earth and influence the collective consciousness of humanity in a positive and beneficial manner.

In this now moment I am at peace. I am one with all that is. I am.

In this now moment my soul finds rest.

In this now moment I let go of my all preoccupation with understanding Earth life and allow my higher self to speak to my mind and join with me in this oneness of the now moment.

In this now moment I am free from worry about what I have or have not done. Setting aside all concerns, releasing all residual thoughts about my day, I simply listen and focus within. There, I find clarity to understand my purpose for being on Earth at this time.

In this now moment there exists no problems, no trouble; there is nothing to worry my mind, for all is love in this moment and love is all there really ever is.

In this now moment I know that whatever tomorrow brings will be pleasant. I will have all the energy and resources I need to fulfill my mission.

In this now moment I feel peaceful. I feel whole. I am peaceful. I am whole.

In this now moment from my heart center I radiate love, light, peace, joy, and harmony.

In this now moment everything is in perfect order.

In this now moment I rest assured that I am on a path to oneness and wholeness.

In this now moment I am one with the light. The light flows through me. The light is in me. The light is me.

In this now moment I am at perfect peace. I am calm.

In this now moment I am aware of my connection to the infinite source of all good.

In this now moment I recognize that I am an empowered being of light.

In this now moment I know that I am one with pure consciousness.

In this now moment I feel safe and protected. I feel assured, calm, and at ease.

In this now moment I accept all the good the universe has intended for me.

In this now moment I begin deep breathing

With each inhale, I bring peace to my thoughts. My thoughts produce emotional and physical responses; therefore, I am consistent in monitoring my thoughts and ensuring that they are loving, peaceful, calm, and empowering.

With this deep breath and in this now moment I send peace to every nerve in my body. I remember to do this whenever I feel fearful or anxious. I know I can easily calm myself using deep breathing.

By inhaling and exhaling with purpose I feel peaceful. I bring in the oxygen that fuels all the processes of my body and calms my entire nervous system.

Through deep breathing I realign my thoughts with higher empowered thoughts and I recognize myself as one with everything.

With this deep breath, I see peace within myself and all around me. This peace grows with each deep breath.

In this now moment and with this deep breath, I am aware that I am greater than all my fears.

With this deep breath, I consciously choose to change my fearful thoughts into positive uplifting thoughts. I am always safe.

As I rest in this now moment, I attune to source energy. I receive guidance. I know that I have everything I need.

In this now moment I bring forth my higher consciousness into this body and anchor this loving, beautiful higher vibration in the Earth plane.

The soul that has chosen this embodiment is connected to my oversoul and all my multidimensional selves and realities. I bring in that all-knowing energy that is love, light, and vibration from pure consciousness. The essence of the I AM presence.

In this unity that I have created in this now moment I effect positive healing and beneficial change in humanity and in the Earth plane.

From this now moment, this place of centeredness, I radiate joy and calmness at all times.

From this place of joyful being, I move forward in the energy of pure consciousness, blessing all by being one with ALL THAT IS.

I acknowledge and embrace the help that is available to me now.

I acknowledge and thank the spirit beings that have been called to assist with the next step on my path of ascension.

When I awake in the morning, this body is well rested.

I awake in the now moment. I carry forth and operate in the infinite presence from a place of heart-centered love.

I radiate joy and peace into the lives of everyone I encounter.

As I anchor the accelerated frequencies of my multidimensional counterparts in this Earth plane I am joyful. I am wellbeing. I am healing. I am love. I am light. I am pure. I am awakened. I am conscious of the higher guidance I am receiving. I am clear knowing. I am clear seeing.

In this now moment I AM

Only love is real. I am love. I am this now moment.

Affirmation to Integrate the Christ Oversoul with the Physical Body

The purpose of this mediation is to allow the Christ oversoul to be activated and merged with the physical body and create one cohesive field of light in the auric field. This will help to anchor and fortify your light body. As you calmly and peacefully integrate and merge the accelerated energy of your Christ oversoul it will begin to manifest in your daily human experience.

I acknowledge my creator who is in me, around me, living as me in human form. I am part of the divine matrix known as God/Goddess and the universe. I honor my place, part, and power in bringing heaven to Earth through my thoughts, feelings, beliefs, and actions. I am one with the divine and its infinite possibilities to change my life and my world.

With this deep inhalation, I breathe love and light into my heart center. This pure, divine essence is expanding and increasing to encompass and clear my throat and solar plexus chakras. I am one with the ALL THAT IS Source flowing through, around, and within me.

With this deep inhalation, I breathe love and light into my heart center. This pure, divine essence is expanding and increasing to encompass and clear my pineal chakra located in the center of my head and my sacral chakra in my abdomen. I am one with the ALL THAT IS Source flowing through, around, and within me.

With this deep inhalation, I breathe love and light into my heart center. This pure, divine essence is expanding and increasing to encompass and clear my crown chakra at the top of my head and my root chakra at the base of my spine. I am one with the ALL THAT IS Source flowing through, around, and within me.

With this deep inhalation, I breathe love and light into my heart center. This pure, divine essence is expanding and increasing to encompass and clear my alpha chakra above my head and my omega chakra located between my thighs. I am one with the ALL THAT IS Source flowing through, around, and within me.

With this deep inhalation, I breathe love and light into my heart center. This pure, divine essence is expanding and increasing to encompass and clear my entire physical body. I am one with the ALL THAT IS Source flowing through, around, and within me.

With this deep inhalation, I allow my Christ oversoul to be activated and merged with all my chakras and my physical body to create one cohesive field of light. Anchoring and fortifying my divine light body on Earth, I calmly and peacefully integrate and merge the accelerated energy of my Christ oversoul into my daily human experience.

With this deep inhalation, I allow my Christ oversoul to be activated and merged with all the subtle auric bodies surrounding my physical body, and create one cohesive field of light. Anchoring and fortifying my divine light body on Earth, I calmly and peacefully integrate and merge the accelerated energies of my Christ oversoul into my daily human experience.

With this deep inhalation, I allow my Christ oversoul, my divine light body, and the ALL THAT IS Source to be activated and merged with all aspects of my being in one cohesive field of light, and radiate through, around, and within my chakras, bodies, aura, and human experience—in all ways and at all times.

And it is so.

Affirmations for Immortality

The mind of the soul reincarnates from one life to another; it never dies. You may have been working on physical immortality in previous lifetimes. If so, you will probably resonate with the thoughts on this page. Perhaps you will achieve it in this lifetime! If not, you are still helping yourself (and humanity) by sending energy to this concept. It's worth a try! What have you got to lose, right? As Leonard Orr says, "Death is a grave mistake!" and "Physical immortality as a living philosophy is the only cause you can't die for!" and "You are immortal until you prove otherwise."

Why prove otherwise? Why not live in a new reality? I find this very exciting and just thinking about it has created more hope in my mind and joy in all the cells of my body. We can begin creating the energy for immortality by talking about it with others and reprogramming our minds with messages about living life to the fullest. Here is an exercise to help you do this.

When I operate in conscious awareness of my life urge, I am joyful, relaxed, and at peace.

All humans have a choice to make regarding how, when, and IF death will occur for them. I allow others to make their own decision about longevity, but I am choosing eternal immortality for my beautiful body.

I enjoy my life and appreciate my own beauty so much, I want to be in my divine physical body on this Earth plane.

114

If I get bored with Earth life, I will simply shift into my light body and visit other places in our wonderful multiverse for a while.

I am in the process of eliminating my unconscious death urge and allowing life to consume every fiber of my being.

I release anything unlike love or life.

I am willing to let go of any thoughts about death or dying.

I can gauge my life urge by how much I love and appreciate and care for myself and my body. The more pleasure and joy I experience, the more my life urge is increasing.

There may be times when certain aspects of the death urge habit come up for healing. I will lovingly acknowledge, release, process, and resolve these issues without resistance to the healing that is being offered to me.

I will realign my thoughts and emotions with the mind of God.

My body is my servant. It does whatever I request according to my beliefs. If something is not satisfactory about my body, I will allow this to serve as a reminder that my mind needs renewing. I will gladly submit my thoughts to the mind of the Christ Consciousness.

I breathe to renew my mind and release my body from the effects of fear-based thoughts.

Because I love my body and myself, I enjoy taking care of my body.

I enjoy bathing my body. The sweet-smelling soap and warm water feel so good!

I enjoy wearing nice clothes that fit well and flatter my beautiful figure.

I find pleasure in exercising and moving my body. Dancing is fun. Walking is refreshing, and I find all kinds of enjoyable activities to engage my body in.

I really like to play and be as free as a child.

I am youthful.

I am youthing!

I am getting younger every day.

My body is overcoming the abuse it withstood when I was not aware of my death urge. Now, I am consciously creating health and well-being for my body and mind.

My body looks and feels ageless as I accumulate innumerable Earth years.

I can relax and take it easy anytime I please. It's great to have fun!

I don't need as much sleep or food now that my body is processing Light as an energy source.

My body feels refreshed no matter how many or few hours I sleep.

My body feels full and satisfied. This allows me to mindfully chew my food and enjoy each healthy bite. This also allows me to fast when I want to increase my spiritual ascension process.

I am immortal.

My body is everlasting.

I call forth life in every cell of my body.

I will emphasize the life urge in all my conversations—both mental and verbal.

I am thrilled when I am having pleasure.

I am ascending in body and spirit.

I can laugh easily—especially when I think of how absurd the death urge is.

I am one with the Life Force that created me.

Life is easy.

I am blessed to be living in an immortal body.

My body has put on incorruption! Thank you, Jesus, for setting the example for me. I love you dearly!

I bless all those who have overcome death, ascended, and shown me the way to physical immortality.

Death has no sting—it does not exist for me. The grave has no victory over my body—I consciously create life with every breath I take.

I am pleased with my spiritual progress. All my spiritual purification techniques have and are working well to rid my body, emotions, and mind of the death urge.

Affirmation for Loving the Body

Your body is in the process of becoming a light body that will never die. Its DNA is being restructured to allow it to bi-locate or dematerialize in one place dimension and rematerialize in another. So, how important is your physical body at this present time? Very important! Are you treating it with love and respect? The amount of love and care you give your body is a direct indication of how much you love yourself. Once you learn to love yourself, loving others is easy.

The body is a vehicle for the soul as it moves about in the 3-D Earth plane. Many people think that the way to ascension is through punishing the body or "dying to the flesh" because that is what the Bible seems to say we are to do. The "flesh" being referred to in that scripture is not the physical body—the body is neutral—what is dying through the ascension process is the ego or separatist mindset that has caused us to suffer and struggle. I compare the biological body to a car. We don't beat a vehicle into submission and force it to take us somewhere. We simply turn the key, and trust it to do its job, safely transporting us from one location to the next. If we maintain the car, it will last for many years and miles. So it is with our physical body. A well-nourished, sufficiently rested, and adequately-exercised body is more likely to achieve healthful longevity and immortality.

Body change begins in the mind and the heart. Reprogram your thoughts with positive affirmations to start loving your entire being as a divine creation!

I love my body.

My body is beautiful, filled with love and light.

I love the way my body feels.

I enjoy caressing my body's soft skin.

My hair, teeth, and nails are beautiful and healthy.

I like the way I look and feel.

My every cell radiates joy, peace, well-being, and happiness.

Because I love myself I will not subject myself to unpleasant or unfulfilling situations.

Each cell of my body accesses divine intelligence to create perfect new cells on an on-going basis.

Every cell in my body is gloriously refreshed with new cells that bring new life—each day, each moment.

I accept myself as I am.

I allow my body proper rest, exercise, and nourishment.

I allow the flow of cosmic life force energy to connect me to the mysteries of the multiverse.

I am amazed at how wonderfully my human body functions. It serves me well!

I am blessed to be living in this lovely, healthy body.

I am fully present in my body.

I am glad to be in a body on Earth at such a wonderful time as this.

I am thankful for the privilege of being able to create the life that I now enjoy.

I create a positive, rewarding experience in this human body.

I enjoy expressing myself sexually. I like the way my body responds to touch.

I have a right to live a pleasant and healthy life.

I have love, compassion, and understanding for myself. My actions support this belief.

I know and adore my body.

I love myself.

I love the life I have created.

I partner with my beautiful body to maintain perfect health.

I trust my body; it knows what to do to stay healthy and it is doing its job to maintain wellness and balance in all its systems and functions.

I use my body most effectively.

My body and its biology operate in divine intelligence.

My body can produce whatever is required to bring about a perfect state of health.

My body is an incredible and intelligent self-healing system.

My body is radiant and filled with sparkling light.

My body is shifting easily and peacefully into a light body. What a beautiful, wonderful process!

My body's DNA is aligned with the higher intelligence of the cosmic mind. This innate wisdom directs each cell, each atom, each molecule to operate flawlessly and exactly as my Creator intended.

My body's natural intelligence communicates from one cell to the next, opening new possibilities for vibrant, vital, energetic well-being and perfect health.

My life is significant and purposeful.

My mental conversation is positive and loving. I'm always reminding myself of how I am a wonderful part of the God-Goddess.

Life force energy sustains me.

Body, I love you. I am thankful for you.

Namaste!

Affirmations for Healing the Physical Body

From time to time we may experience an episode in which the body seems to malfunction. Illness and dis-ease is your body's way of communicating that something needs to change. We do well to listen to our body and treat it kindly.

 The physical body is influenced by whatever signals the mind, emotions, and subconscious beliefs transmit. If we hold a lot of anger or fear in our emotional body, it can show up as discomfort or sickness in the physical body. In order to heal the physical body, we need to make adjustments to the energetic template created by our thoughts and emotions. Used daily, affirmations are one way of altering that template.

I am healing myself now.

I love and appreciate my body.

I am thankful for a healthy body that has served me well all these years.

I accept myself and my body as I am.

I have created all I am encountering now. I have created it in order to discover my personal power and learn to make choices that liberate my spirit from endless loops of despair.

I accept the responsibility and commitment that changing my life and health may involve. I embrace a new way of looking at life.

Any traumatic events or unfinished business is now resolved with peace, forgiveness, and understanding. I have learned the lessons that these were intended to bring. There is no longer a need for these impressions or imprints to be on any of my body's cells or cellular memory.

I consciously and deliberately let go of anything that has held back my healing.

Forgiveness is the ultimate act of letting go. I forgive all, freeing myself and others from the endless cycle of guilt and blame.

I affirm that I am a vital healthy being now.

I allot time each day to quiet my mind so I may discover how to successfully integrate the accelerated, pure energy from Source. This keeps my nervous system in balance.

I allow my body proper rest, exercise, and nourishment.

I am excited about learning the many methods and techniques that will empower me to operate my physical body and experience vital health in every moment.

I am getting in better form day by day, year by year, decade by decade.

I am healing and I am a healer.

I am healing the patterns of misplaced intent in my bloodline.

I am healing all genetic misinformation in my DNA. The patterns for healing my body are now activated in my genes.

I am open to change.

I am releasing all patterns of confusion and despair that have affected my current state of health.

I am thankful for the privilege of being able to create the life that I now enjoy.

I am transforming my health.

I am willing to deal with anything that needs to be healed.

I am willing to feel whatever I need to feel in order to heal. I take on this task with my higher guidance and God's wisdom so I can heal and clear every issue with harmonious resolution.

I ask from a self-empowered point of view: "What unresolved issues am I dealing with? Why is this illness or discomfort in my life? What contribution have my thoughts made to this process? What is the overall spiritual lesson and purpose for this experience?"

I change my actions and beliefs to create a harmonious resolution for any disempowering states of guilt or blame.

I choose love and well-being.

I am fortified with the courage to meet my fears and resolve them.

I create a quality life by transcending past limitations.

I choose to activate the best possibilities.

I achieve my greatest victories by suspending judgment and abandoning victimhood.

I seek the greater meaning of life.

I choose the codes of consciousness that best express my life as a multidimensional light being filled with love, connected to the radiate cosmic energy that creates life at all levels.

I claim my divine power now.

I do emotional clearing on a regular basis. The accelerated energy that is here to assist me now is being calmly, peacefully, and healthfully integrated with all dimensions of my body, soul, and mind—now, in past lives, and forever.

I establish healthy boundaries and respect the boundaries of others as I learn how to manage my own energy. I am able to be myself even when around others, without being adversely affected by their misuse of energy.

I exercise my free will and mental power to change my health. I choose perfect and divine health for every cell, system, and function in my body.

I respect the lessons of others and allow them to choose their own course. I will not be dragged down by their negativity.

When I'm around others who are negative I will remember to relax and breathe in life-enhancing light deep into my body—even to the subatomic level. I can only change myself.

There is nothing in me or my electromagnetic field that can create stickiness for anything negative or detrimental to adhere to.

I am an inspiration to others who appear to be resistant to change.

I have clarity of mind.

I feel tremendous gratitude for the courage to heal myself.

I have a right to live a pleasant, prosperous, and healthy life.

I have the power to change my attitude and beliefs to heal myself. It can be as simple as recognizing self-pity and changing it to self-acceptance.

I ask my guides for help with changing anger and pain to forgiveness and joy.

I produce the vibration of healing love.

I expect results as I allow the process of healing to have its due course.

I let go of bitterness, anger, wounds, or death trauma carried over from other life times.

I let go of any violence, sexual misconduct, or other invasive experiences that may have marred my self-esteem. I no longer replay the same old damaging story line. Instead, I develop a greater vision of who I am and choose a better outcome in all areas of my life.

I love and appreciate my body. I express this love through healthy eating habits and activities that nurture and support optimal health.

I now act in favor of my own well-being.

I release and let go of patterns stored in my genes that hold memories of my various incarnations. I transmute the sad story of my genetic bloodline. I am not a victim! I am empowered. I say yes to new ways of experiencing my wonderful life.

I respond to my body's messages that signal me to change my beliefs and attitudes and improve my health and every aspect of my life.

I understand that my ultimate responsibility is to love and care for my physical body as I manage my own decisions, life, and health.

It is not natural for my body to be ill; therefore, I do not expect pain or suffering.

To have any of symptoms of sickness simply means my body is obeying a subconscious command given by my mind. That's okay; I can change my mind and reprogram it to think in line with God's mind. Improved health will quickly follow.

Life force energy sustains me.

Life is well worth living. I am healthy.

My body is gently assisting me as I direct it on a new course of action.

My body works with me. It is designed to respond to my thoughts, beliefs, and emotions.

My body thrives on the energy of love that I feel for myself. I affirm and act as if I am worthy of my own love.

My cells, molecules, atoms, and subatomic particles intelligently communicate with one another. Their job is to respond to my mental and emotional input.

My life is significant and purposeful.

My new mindset for perfect health is being purposefully developed to override any messages of despair that have signaled my body to malfunction.

I now focus on replacing unproductive attitudes and changing my interpretation of my body's messages.

I open my heart with the intention of healing whatever has hurt me.

The healing I seek is already available.

Each healing phase is short, easy, and sweet. Everything works out just fine in a remarkable series of beneficial events.

> *When I heal myself, I heal all my relations on all lines of time.*
>
> *I am healed now.*
>
> *I love my beautiful body.*

Repeating Mantras Using Prayer Beads

I wasn't raised Catholic, but I have found truth in all religions and spiritual traditions. Repeating mantras or affirmations while using prayer beads is very effective. Touching each bead on the strand as I repeat an uplifting and empowering phrase keeps my focus on what I am saying and sends that energy into the cellular memory of my physical body. You can purchase a rosary or use a beaded necklace as I do.

Embracing Divine Feminine Energy

The Divine Mother is known by many names in all religions and traditions. In Christianity, she is the Virgin Mary. In Hawaii, she is Pele. In China, she is Quan Yin. In India, she is represented by Shakti and many other goddesses. Many of the goddesses of Pagan religions,, such as Wicca come from Greek/Roman mythology. Regardless of what you call Her or what religious path you follow, the Divine Mother can be a nurturing presence and a powerful guide during your ascension process.

Men and women possess both the masculine and feminine aspects of the divine. In each individual one aspect is typically expressed more than the other. What we want to achieve is a balance of both these energies. Since there has been an excess of masculine energy in the male-dominant patriarchal system under which we have lived for thousands of years, it is necessary to bring more divine feminine energy into our lives and onto this planet just to tip the scales toward equilibrium.

In a patriarchal system, the strongest or wealthiest person is at the top of the pyramid. Those who are more vulnerable are crushed under the weight of the pyramid; so, they either submit or they are ignored/eliminated. A system heavy with masculine energy is very linear (i.e.: we are mental creatures, who just happen to live in a body), controlling, and greed-based, as seen in the operation of banks, governments, the Federal Reserve, huge pharmaceutical companies, and the stock market. We put our money and our faith into a system because we want to be able to take care of ourselves when we reach retirement age. We could be investing in a matriarchal system or "global village mindset" where everyone— especially elders—is valued and cared for. These are two very different ways of taking care of people as they age. One is built on self-sufficiency and the other is built on community.

Fear-driven patriarchal systems are currently going through shock and starting to crumble as the Divine Mother energy is arising on Earth. We are shifting to a matriarchal system where there is consideration for every person and each person has an equal voice. Rather than controlling others, we are beginning to honor a sense of community in which we rely on gifts of intuition and share in order to meet one another's needs.

There are several books I recommend to help you better understand why the divine feminine energy must arise as part of the ascension process. *Anna, Grandmother of Jesus* by Claire Heartsong brings illumination to the sacred philosophies and teachings of the concealed Essene community of which Jesus Christ (Yeshua ben Joseph) was an initiate. Heartsong offers mystical insight into how the "light-conceived" Jesus acquired the knowledge and power to perform miracles, including raising His physical body after being in the tomb for three days. The mysteriously "lost years" of Jesus are lost only in the Bible, which has been altered by patriarchal "powers that be" in order to gain control of the masses throughout the years. Other historical documents recently unearthed demonstrate Jesus' presence in Egypt, England, India, Italy, and throughout the Mediterranean. This book revolutionized my understanding of the life and ministry of Jesus. I fell in love with Him in a totally new way after reading it.

Rock Your World with the Divine Mother by Sondra Ray is another excellent read. In chapter 12, she gives a prayer honoring the 108 names of the Divine Mother. I have created my own version of a similar prayer to invoke the presence of the Divine Mother. I invite you to listen to the MP3 "Divine Mother Puja" at http://weare1inspirit.com/spiritual-audios.htm or create your own version.

Opening the Heart to Receive

Each person has three hearts—the trinity of human spirituality. These are defined as I see them:

1. The **physical heart** supports the physical body. It's the organ that pumps and circulates blood throughout the body. The heart chakra is a reception site for the energy coming from the spiritual heart.

2. The **spiritual heart** connects us to a dimension of pure, spiritual awareness or unconditional love, which is free of mental and emotional influences. The spiritual heart is also the center of creativity.

3. Connecting the physical heart to the spiritual heart is the **Sacred Heart** (God, All That Is) that supports the electromagnetic energy field of the brain/body. It is where true prayer (or communion with our creator) resides. This is our true essence!

The spiritual heart is how we connect to the divine within us and heal any aspect of ourselves that has fragmented. Reconnecting with the Sacred Heart allows you to become aware of your authentic self that easily experiences love, peace, and joy. You have not forgotten your union with the Sacred Heart; your human perspective in this 3-D world may have caused you to see yourself as separate from it.

When your spiritual heart is connected to your Sacred Heart, you are in a state of truth and you live authentically. Your heart is open yet you are not worried about being hurt because you intuitively know what and who you can trust and you know what doesn't resonate with your personal truth. When you have absolute connection to Spirit you have clear guidance and feel totally peaceful.

When your heart is closed to love, you may feel sad, alone, depressed, abandoned, or rejected. Because the heart communicates through your feelings and emotions, these feelings are your heart's way of telling you that it does not feel connected to Source. When the heart is walled off from Source, it can create all sorts of problems in relationships as well as in the physical body—especially with the physical heart.

We need to love ourselves before we can love anyone else, and this self-love comes from the Sacred Heart. When we depend upon a relationship or another person to make us feel loved and that person is suddenly gone from our lives, we may feel hopeless. This is when we *really* need to give ourselves unconditional love, emotional support, self-respect, and adoration. It is very important to reconnect with the Sacred Heart and do or be for yourself what the partner had been. In other words, we pick up the role that person was playing and we become our own lover. When you are feeling lost or lonely, let it serve as a reminder to look within and find sacred love. When you are whole in and of yourself, you are ready to share your heart in a relationship that fully supports you and your partner.

Being in a close relationship with another person gives us the opportunity to share love that comes from the Sacred Heart, but it cannot replace our divine connection with the source of love. You can count on the Sacred Heart to always be there. It dwells within you forever.

When the heart is connected, miracles can happen. The body becomes healthy and life situations improve. Dreams, pure thoughts, enlightening visions, and limitless possibilities streaming from the Sacred Heart create positive changes that truly serve our oneness and support the shift we are making as a species.

When you are operating from the Sacred Heart space, you radiate love from every pore of your body. This causes the cells of your physical body to be filled with light (spirit). When you are joined with the light, all sickness and death are erased from the cellular memory of your body and it becomes immortal. Death is overcome. Your flesh becomes spirit. This is the second birth. This is what it means to be born again.

When we make decisions only through the mind, we have multiple problems. When our decisions come from the heart, we have clear direction and make decisions from a place of clear knowing and clear seeing. In the Sacred Heart we have all the resources we need to make our lives enjoyable and easy. When we live from a place of heart-centeredness, we see and understand the big picture of life. Then, our heart is filled with a deep sense of confidence and trust. It is when we believe and live as if we are separated from this Sacred Heart that we begin to create by default (without purposeful intention) and bring unpleasant things into our lives. The logical mind would have us believe that we don't have what we need or that there is lack.

The goal of the heart-centered meditation that I co-created with Dr. Caron Goode is to reunite your spiritual heart with the Sacred Heart and increase your awareness of the love and wisdom of higher realms. I'm amazed at the peace and calm I feel whenever I do this exercise. To know that your soul is infused with love and to feel the joy of living in union with the I AM presence brings true healing and a revelation of our future selves—the ascended version of our soul. In that rendition, the heaviness, fatigue, discomfort, or illness you may be experiencing now does not exist. The energy for helping making this shift is here now.

Heart-Centered Meditation

I affirm that I am centered, aligned, and heart wise, and I intend through this focused meditation to open my heart, will, and clear knowing.

Breathing in and breathing out, I am aligning my heart, will, and clear knowing with the alpha and with the omega. I am aligned.

Placing my right hand on my heart and gently inhaling...exhaling... inhaling...exhaling... I focus on my heart center. I go inward to heart... I am in heart, and I rest my awareness there.

Breathing in slowly... and illuminating my heart, filling my heart with crystalline white light. With each breath I take, the white light is brighter and whiter, growing and filling my heart.

Centered in my heart and aligned, each time I inhale, I send rays of my white light swirling through my body, around my body, and through the soles of my feet to the Earth for a solid, grounded connection.

My heart glows with warmth and wisdom. My heart light beams its brilliance outward, forward, preparing my path. The rays of heart light open doors of opportunity, clear my way, and enhance my clear knowing.

I am centered, aligned, and heart wise. I am centered in my heart, aligned in my will, and clear in my awareness.

I trust the heart's wisdom, listen to the heart's passions, and feel the calm, serene space within.

I Am.

Using Incense or Smudging with Sage

The healing of the body (nations, world) is in the leaves of plants. A plant-based diet is effective not only for maintaining excellent physical health, but in reconnecting with the Earth and the divine feminine energy. Plants have medicine, chemical properties, and an energetic vibration; some are higher and more healing than others. The centuries-old practice of smudging with herbs is very effective in clearing your auric field and driving away negativity while helping to ground your energy. The sage plant (often used by Native Americans) can cleanse, sterilize, re-energize, or fix the vibrational level of just about anything. Therefore, it is my go-to when I need to clear negative thought forms.

There are many methods that work when used with reverence. When you smudge, you are asking the spirit of sacred plants for assistance. Basically, you add dried sage, sweetgrass, lavender, juniper, rosemary, or cedar (I've even used tobacco) to a heat-proof bowl and light the leaves/stems to create an aromatic smoke bath. One person directs this smoke to cover the body and aura of another person.

Many people asked me if this Native American technique could be done if you don't have a partner to assist you. Since we are living in a time of integration where all paths are honored and merged, I see no reason why one must follow a strict regime of "getting it right" (indicative of a patriarchal system). It is our intention that counts. Each purification effort we make supports the grid of light surrounding the Earth and helps anchor pure spirit essence for the individual and collective consciousness (group mind). I created a video to demonstrate how to smudge yourself with sage. Click the video tab on my website: http://weare1inspirit.com/spiritual-videos.htm.

Epsom Salt and Alcohol Home-Clearing Recipe

Most people are unaware of non-physical entities that can actively interfere with the energy, emotions, and atmosphere of a person, house, or room. However, the more you purify your thoughts, the more aware you are going to become of what's going on energetically around you. You will quickly notice when something is not right in your home or energy field. If you sense that your home has some unpleasant energy, you can shift it with the following technique.

Epsom salt has a crystalline molecular structure, which is opened when heated. There's a very simple technique that clears from your home imprints from your thoughts and emotions. It gives you a clean foundation to build protective forces that will prevent ghosts or spirit attachments from having an impact on your home. It's kind of like vacuuming the mental, emotional, and psychic environment of your home. It's a good idea to do this exercise once a month. Maybe more, depending on what's going on. Use this method very carefully and in a safe place.

- Select a large pot with a cover. Place the pot either on the stove or in your kitchen sink and make sure nothing flammable (like kitchen curtains) is above it. It's a good idea to have a Class C fire extinguisher close by. Better to have it and not need it than need it and not have it. You also want to keep children and pets away from the area while you're performing this clearing.

- Make sure that the interior of the pot is dry. Add about one tablespoon of regular Epsom salt and cover that with about four tablespoons of rubbing alcohol. Be careful how much alcohol you add, because that will determine how long this combination is going to burn.

- Light a wooden match (*not* a lighter), step back, and gently drop the lit match into the pot. The flames will usually flash higher than the sides of the pot. That's why you have it in the sink and are *not* walking around the house with it. The alcohol will ignite and burn for a few minutes. You will feel the energy in the room go flat or cold.

- After the flames have died down, place the cover over the pot; allow the pot to cool before you touch it.

Calling the Sacred Circle

Common to many Earth-aligned traditions is the use of a circle to "set the stage" or dedicate an area as a sacred space. Like ringing the bell in a church tower, casting a circle indicates that a sacred event is about to begin. While some religions rely on the use of a building such as a church or temple to hold worship, those who honor an Earth-based or goddess-centered religion may cast a circle pretty much any place they choose.

A circle can hold positive energy in or keep unwanted energy out. It can be cast with great effort using ceremonial gear, but many simply acknowledge the elements (air, fire, water, earth) and the four directions while visualizing a circle being drawn around them. Whatever method you choose is fine. What matters is your intention to designate a period of time in a sanctified space to connect with the Divine. You can call the circle prior to meditation or any ritual. I've found that when I call the circle, I'm less distracted. You may find that your phone doesn't even ring to disturb you while you are inside your private circle!

Candle Rituals

Who doesn't love the warm glow of a candle? It creates ambiance and calmness. You can use a candle with any ritual to bring conscious awareness to a situation that needs to be aligned with a purer vibration. I like to use a candle as part of my meditation because staring into the flame helps me focus and enter an altered state of awareness. The ritual itself serves as a calendar event or mental marker, signifying your intention to end an old practice and begin a new belief about a particular thought pattern. A ritual is also a personal request for divine help, so conduct it whenever you need guidance from a higher source.

There is no set manner or prescribed formula that you must follow for your candle ritual. The candle doesn't have to be a certain color; the session need not be performed on the full/new moon or at a particular time of month or day. If you are being led to conduct a ritual, trust that the energy you need is available.

You may have other methods you like better, but here are some basic steps that I use.

- Choose a candle. When it comes to choosing a candle, don't be thrown by the formulas assigned to certain colors such as black for banishing and white for clearing. If you are drawn to a particular color or only have a limited choice, go with whatever suits you at the time.

- You may use a pencil or sharp tool to inscribe on the candle words such as love, peace, resolution, or whatever you desire that day. Simply state what you want to occur as a result of your ritual. The energy will follow your intention.

- Light the candle and take a few deep breaths to quiet your mind.

- Call upon whatever angel, archangel, holy person, ascended master, or light being with whom you resonate. Ask for your higher self and spiritual guidance to assist you with meeting the need at hand.

- Listen to your inner guidance to see if there is a comforting message or action you need to take. Write down what you receive.

- Make your requests known.

- Thank your guides and extinguish your candle or let it burn out on its own. All these rules about not blowing out the candle are wives' tales. You can blow it out or snuff it— whatever suits you.

Be sure to follow through with the message you received during the ritual. Don't worry if you didn't hear or see anything. The message may come later, so look for signs you may be given in the next few days or weeks.

Conscious Breathing

Breathing is the life force that rejuvenates every cell in your body, every activity of your awareness, and every action that you make. Yoga masters knew from ancient times that the breath is the most essential part of human life because it connects us to the life force in all matter. They called this energy by several names, such as prana, chi, ki, or qi. The breath is also what unites us as living beings. The practice of conscious breathing costs nothing and is universal—there is no dogma associated with it, and no religion or government regulating its use! Breathing can be done automatically without thinking about it, but it can also be monitored or controlled consciously in order to achieve physical, emotional, mental, and spiritual benefits.

The lungs are sponge-like tissues inside the bones of the rib cage. Inhaling oxygen increases energy as the lungs absorb oxygen from the air and send it to the blood for transport throughout the body. Exhaling expels byproducts of metabolism as the lungs receive carbon dioxide from the blood and send it out of the body. According to Dr. Tom Goode in his book, *Breathe and Grow Rich*, "Most people in Western society are shallow breathers, breathing in the upper one-third to one-fourth of their lungs. We call this thoracic, or chest breathing. This shallow breathing promotes stress and drains the energy needed for optimal health and vitality."

Purification practices, such as deep breathing, clear our chakras and auric bodies while energizing the physical body and removing toxins from its cells. Breathing is not only a life-giving process; it also has a way of exposing negative and self-destructive patterns. It may bring up issues to be healed, but remember that your focus is on integration. Don't allow yourself to obsess over whatever is stirred up.

Rapid or slow cycles, shallow or deep, nose or mouth, holding the breath or moving air without pausing—there seems to be no limit to the number of methods that can be used for conscious breathing. Each method has different effects and purposes. I will briefly outline those that I am most familiar with. There are many, many other effective techniques; so, I encourage you to find one that resonates with you and diligently use it.

Full-Wave Breathing

Full-Wave Breathing encompasses the benefits of many other types of breathing and, most importantly, returns the integrity of the breathing system to the individual. Full-Wave Breathing has three steps, which affect the abdomen, belly, and chest. The breath starts by inhaling all the way in the abdomen, and then it expands into the belly, and finally into the chest. The exhale allows the air to be released in reverse: chest, belly, abdomen. Nostril breathing is the most natural way to breathe; however, mouth breathing takes in 50 percent more oxygen. Full-Wave Breathing is performed with mouth open until the technique is learned, but you may use nostrils if you prefer. Visit www.fullwavebreathing.com for more information. Full-Wave Breathing is demonstrated by Dr. Tom Goode on his YouTube channel: http://youtu.be/9frOB16m-yw.

Liberation Breathing

You may have heard of rebirthing back in the 1970s, when it was discovered by Leonard Orr. Another pioneer of the rebirthing movement is my dear friend, Sondra Ray, who has demonstrated how our birth experience tremendously impacts our lives. Originally, rebirthers discovered that subconscious memories—in many cases all the way back to birth—could be accessed through deep circular breathing.

The rebirthing technique Sondra teaches today employs Liberation Breathing®, which is a modern-day version of Pranic breathing that helps people to clear limiting thoughts and negative memories. This open-mouth, fast-paced breath uses mostly the upper part of the lungs. This special technique is best done with a Liberation Breathing® facilitator who is trained to guide and support your breathing in a way that enables you to process what occurs during the session. See https://www.liberationbreathing.com to find someone in your area.

Throat Friction Breathing

Throat friction breathing is a technique that activates the throat's energy center (5th chakra) and quiets the mind rather quickly. I first learned about throat friction breathing in Ethan Vorly's e-book, *Tantric Secrets*, and found that it was the easiest method for me to master personally.

Here's how to do it:

- Place your tongue against the roof of your mouth just behind the teeth.

- While inhaling, hold the mouth open slightly and breathe deep, filling the chest and lower abdomen.

- Exhale the breath, pushing air against the back of the throat. The rasping that resonates from it sounds like Darth Vader!

The breath will automatically find its own slow, relaxed rhythm. You will feel centered and present in your body. While your mind is quiet you will be able to sense your inner guidance.

Yogic Breathing

There are many types of yogic breathing and I won't attempt to mention all of them. Basically, here is how it works for beginners:

Sit with legs crossed and your spine erect, extending the crown of your head toward the ceiling. Place the palm of one hand on your heart and the other on your naval. Breathe in slowly through the nose and bring the air all the way into the abdomen then expand it to the rib cage and finally the upper chest. Hold it for a few seconds, and then exhale through the nose, feeling the air leave the abdomen first, following it up the body to the upper chest for full release.

Do as One

Regardless of what type of breathing technique you choose, try adding your focused intent to the energy of others in the breathing rooms on http://doasone.org. Do As One has thirteen rooms including a Universal Meditation Room, a Universal Breathing Room, a Meditation Room, and a Universal Om Room. People all over the world can connect using any type of conscious breathing technique and send focused intention into the world, twenty-four hours a day, seven days a week. As you know there is power in numbers and the more people we have focusing their energy in the same direction, the more and faster results we will see toward world peace. I encourage you to participate whenever you can.

Being Non-Resistant

In my book for empaths (whosestuffisthis.com), I mentioned being non-resistant as a way to manage the energy that you pick up in the environment and from others. This practice of allowing has become even more important and helpful to me as I evolve on my spiritual path.

During his presentation in our telesummit, "Empaths Shifting into 2012," Dr. Tom Goode mentioned four steps to integration that I'd like to share with you now.

Step 1 is Acceptance. When you experience an illness or disease, the first step is to realize that you are one with this condition. It is fruitless to attempt to get rid of, release, drop, or chop off pieces of ourselves. Remember that energy cannot be destroyed or created, it can only be transmuted. Its form can be changed. So struggling against what *is* doesn't work.

The alternative is to integrate. Exhibit no resistance by simply noticing what is going on. Acknowledge the condition and admit you have a [cold, disease, whatever]. There's no need to fight against it. Instead, embrace it, and do everything possible to address the topic. For example, if you have a cold, you can take zinc or vitamin C, drink fluids, rest, stay warm, or whatever it takes to bring the greatest comfort and ease to the physical body.

Expect to deal with your ego mind and emotions. You may find yourself thinking things like *Did I get this cold because I have been bad? Is this a punishment? Is this something that I have brought on myself? What have I done wrong?* Instead of condemning yourself, ask if perhaps you have been pushing yourself too hard and the body is asking for more rest. Pain and *dis*-ease are messages and we are wise to listen to our body. While resting during your recovery, you can catch up on your reading, pick up your email, or talk by phone with someone you haven't visited with for a while. When you're at the end of an "adventure," you can celebrate the healing that took place.

Step 2 is Allowance of the emotional reactions you are having to this condition so there's no denial. Surrender to it, because until you accept what is going on and you're emotionally okay with it, you have no power to change it. That which we resist, will persist. Instead, we must take it in and transmute it. And maybe even transcend it.

My friend, Dr. Tom Goode, told me about the time when he went to the doctor for a checkup and the blood work showed that his body had become diabetic. Immediately he thought of the comorbidities associated with this health condition: loss of vision, loss of limbs, shortened life, heart problems, circulatory problems, etc. *How can this happen?* Tom wondered. *I've always been a healthy guy and never had a problem because of the care I have been taking of the mind-body-spirit system.*

Nevertheless, Tom accepted the condition and allowed it to be there. After all, you can't deny the blood work and the symptoms. He surrendered to the fact that his body had a condition that had come about for reasons unknown. Realizing there was something in his life that needed addressing, he passed through acceptance and allowance pretty quickly and got to the next step—embracement.

Step 3 is Embracement. *How can I embrace this thing?* Tom thought. *This disease is terminal and progressive. It has no cure according to traditional medical models.* The doctor gave him drugs but Tom decided to do everything necessary to embrace this condition instead. He minded the suggested dietary regimens. He researched Asian, Indian, European, and western medicines to see what herbs, supplements, vitamins, etc. could be brought to bear. And, realizing that we change every night, he continued to practice the Full-Wave Breathing he had been using since he created the technique more than thirty years ago.

Before arising each morning, for twelve to fifteen minutes, he used his breath to align with the energies of the day, prepare to see miracles, and see himself as a spiritual being. Placing his hand on his lower abdomen beneath the naval and with his mouth open (to increase oxygen flow) he inhaled and pushed his belly up and then relaxed. With all the emphasis and effort directed toward the inhale, he imagined breathing in light, love, joy, peace, harmony, balance, ease, exuberance, and enthusiasm. He thought of every affirmation and feel-good thought he knew. All the while, he allowed for everything to be different, embracing the fact that this condition was a new opportunity for growth and celebration. As each day ended, he allowed for all the things that were done and not done to be set aside as he again practiced Full-Wave Breathing.

Step 4 is Celebrating. Tom went back to his medical practitioner four months later. The doctor said, "You can stop taking the drugs. There is no diabetic condition present."

"Good!" Tom said, "I never started taking them." This miracle had been accomplished through the integration process: acceptance, allowance, embracement, and celebration.

Rather than resisting the birthing (resurrection) process we are going through, I invite you to follow Tom's suggestions and relax in divine love and allow every cell in your body to know and accept union with its creator.

Prayer

Prayer has been proven to be effective throughout history. Then, why is it some prayers work while others fail? In his book, *Secrets of the Lost Mode of Prayer*, Gregg Braden relates that "The Lord's Prayer" contains a formula that has been lost in our Western thinking. This "vibratory technology" is very effective in producing great results from prayer.

Prayer is not the same as begging God for a favor. When I was in Christian prayer circles almost everyone prayed with a statement such as "If it be thy will" or "Dear God, please do this or that." This type of pleading suggests that what you want is not what God wants for you or another person. I've since learned that God isn't sitting on a throne somewhere out there deciding who is worthy of having a favor granted. Thanks to the law of attraction, we always get whatever we are aligned with energetically. When we carry pure thoughts and emotions, we vibrate in alignment with the Divine Plan and we can simply speak forth our desires. Jesus commanded with clarity what he wanted to transpire: "Be healed!" or "Lazarus, come forth!" and it happened instantly. Jesus said that we could do even greater things than He did. We simply must have the same mind (pure thoughts) and faith that He did.

The laws of the universe work for everyone and the answer to our prayer is always *yes!* Unfortunately, that means that we many times get what we don't want because we are creating by default (unconsciously). We attract to ourselves whatever our emotions, thoughts, and hidden beliefs send out as a prayer. One universal law grants that whatever you focus on will increase. So, it is important that you do not dwell on the lack of something or give energy to what you don't want to manifest. By doing so, you actually create more of the conditions that you don't want! It's not hard to pray without ceasing. Everything we say, think, or feel is a prayer. Yikes!

You can engage in prayer to God, Goddess, the Holy Spirit, saints, angels, archangels, ascended masters, and other spiritual helpers because we are all one in spirit. The thing that counts is a heart-felt desire to connect with God-Goddess to bring about a desired action that aligns with the Divine Plan to bring Heaven to Earth. Prayer is a lifestyle carried out in state of consciousness. Once you learn to master this level of consciousness, the words you speak in faith with clarity and positive emotions will come forth faster and faster. If you want to study the scientific formula behind effective prayer, I suggest you read Susan Shumsky's book, *Miracle Prayer: Nine Steps to Creating Prayers That Get Results*.

Feelings and Emotions

Have you noticed that the time it takes between desiring something and then seeing it manifest is shorter than it used to be? This is a result of the shift we are currently participating in. The energy is here for acceleration of everything. Everything is energy, including our thoughts—even our prayers; therefore, everything we see is a projection of our thoughts and feelings. The difference in lip service and heart service in prayer is the faith and energy of your feelings and emotions.

Words that do not come from the heart are empty. Mankind has uttered millions of words that have had little effect. So, if you want to take your manifestation ability to the next level and *really* see results, you'll need to do more than just speak. Feelings,

> "As a man thinketh in his heart, so is he."
>
> ~ Proverbs 23:7

beliefs, and emotions are powerful. When you believe that you have what you want when you speak prayers/affirmations with feelings of gratitude, hope, love, joy, or any emotion, it fuels your words and creates a shift in energy that will produce results. It raises your consciousness to a meaningful level and expresses a sincere desire of the heart, which connects with the co-creative power of the universe. The more energetically charged your prayer/affirmation, the faster it will be answered.

Clarity

When praying, state clearly and visualize what you want to manifest. Feel free to use the "Statement of Clear Intent" given later in this chapter. Describe your request in the present tense as if your prayer has already been answered. Call those things that are not yet manifested,

> Call those things that be not as though they were.
>
> ~ Romans 4:17

as though they were already here. For example: I am healthy and whole. I am wealthy and prosperous. I am toned and fit at my ideal weight of ____ pounds. Adding details without giving criteria for fulfillment (must be done this way, at this time, by this person, etc.) is good!

Shift your focus onto what you want to create—not just on the things you want to draw to yourself, but to also recognize yourself as a magnificent empowered being and live from that confident perspective. Remember, if you are focused on what is wrong, that's what you will get more of. The more you focus on your desired intention, the faster a positive change will manifest for you. When you start to worry or feel depressed, use this statement of clear intent to get your mind and feelings back on track.

Statement of Clear Intent

Begin by grounding and centering your energy. If you are unsure of how to do this, see the "Grounding and Centering" exercise in this chapter. Then, focus on the Sacred Heart within you (taught in this chapter), knowing that all is well. There are no problems in the now moment. With this in mind, begin to feel in your body what it would feel like if you had everything you need or want right now. That feeling activates the energy of unlimited potential. This is very powerful when combined with positive affirmations.

Call upon your higher self and divine guides as you write a statement of clear intention in the form of affirmations regarding the situation at hand. Keep your affirmations open-ended. For example: To say "I want a job or roommate to help pay the bills" limits what the universe can bring you. It is more helpful to state "I enjoy financial freedom" or "I have all I need to live comfortably."

Here are some other examples:

I have unlimited resources.

Everything I need comes to me in perfect timing.

I am successful in all my ventures.

I am supported by the universe who always says YES!

I attract people into my life who are confident, content, and intelligent.

I express and show happiness easily and freely .

I feel confident in my body.

I receive income from multiple sources.

I receive pure love and support from all.

Sometimes people get so overwhelmed with trouble, disappointment, and frustration they can't even think straight to put together a list like this one. If you have trouble thinking of what you want to manifest, make a list of everything that is *wrong* or that you *don't want* then write the opposite as a positive statement.

Trust

Once you make your request, believe that you have received what you asked for. Rather than undo the creation process with negative words like "I probably won't get _____." Instead, speak positively as if the result is already manifested: "I am vibrantly healthy," or "I am well now." You may not have lived long enough to see the results, but the

> Whatever you ask for in prayer, believe that you have received it, and it will be yours.
>
> ~ Mark 11:23-24

answer is being supplied and is forming. Even though there may not yet be any material evidence that the prayer had been answered, allow yourself to feel the feeling as if the prayer of healing is already done or the desire is already fulfilled. Thankfulness goes a long way in convincing your mind that your prayers have been answered.

In *Find and Use Your Inner Power*, Emmet Fox suggests we "treat the treatment" rather than asking again and again for the same thing. Instead, remind yourself of the spiritual truth concerning it. This is where affirmations come into play. They powerfully state with gratitude the belief that you already have what you asked for during your prayer session. Mr. Fox says, "Claim that God worked through you when you gave the treatment (prayer) and that God's work must succeed. Insist that your treatment, being a Divine activity, cannot be hindered by any seeming difficulties or material conditions."

Become an observer detached from the outcome as you watch your prayer unfold. Let go of the notion that the answer will happen in any particular way or certain time. Because of your attitude of certainty, and gratitude, the fulfillment of your prayer will take form in perfect and divine order.

> Ask and it will be given to you: seek and you will find: knock and the door will be opened to you.
>
> ~ Mathew 7:7

The prayers for things that affect the fewest number of people are the easiest ones to manifest. When others are involved, so is their free will and energy, which may not be aligned with your intention or the Divine Plan. You can always send love and light to another person—this only helps bring clarity and positive energy—but it's futile to pray for change in a person's life if he or she has not desired it. Trust that their soul is arranging events and conditions to help it ascend. Our connectedness with the light means that we are all moving in the same direction, wanting the same thing: for the Earth and humanity to ascend as quickly and peacefully as possible. Praying for world peace involves everyone on the planet. The answer to this prayer may not come immediately but it *is* coming through the shift, and it will manifest as more and more people join the energy of their prayers and emotions to the cause.

Entity Release Prayer

Having discovered an entity attached to the auric field of a person, it is simple to remove it with the help of the angels, archangels, or ascended masters. Try this on yourself before you administer it to others. Do *not* violate the free will of another person, or attempt to remove an entity from anyone who is not aware of what you are doing, or has not given permission for this to be done. This will only aggravate the entity and make it more aggressive.

Lighting a candle, incense, or sage can enhance the following practice to release an earthbound entity.

1. Call upon Archangel Michael to detach and remove the earthbound entity from the human's field and prevent the spirit from influencing the human again.

2. Ask Archangels Azrael and Chamuel to help the earthbound soul cross into the Light where it may begin the next phase of soul development.

3. Depending upon how long the entity has been in place, detachment could create a hole in the auric field of the host human. Call for Archangel Raphael to bring his healing emerald green light and fill the hole and any gaps or tears left by the departed entity.

4. Ask Archangel Michael to clear, seal, and protect the entire aura and allow it to heal without further invasion.

5. Ask that Archangel Uriel assist with keeping the aura healthy and whole. Thank Archangels Michael, Azrael, Chamuel, Raphael, and Uriel for their assistance.

Ascension Prayer

Notice how many affirmations are used in this next prayer. That's because we know that the Divine Plan supports our ascension and all its processes. There's no need to ask for this; simply affirm it is so. This prayer has been set to music and is available on my Website, weare1inspirit.com.

As I seek the stillness within my own heart in this now moment, I acknowledge my creator whose holographic image is in me, reflecting around me, and expressing as me in human form. I am part of the divine matrix known as ALL THAT IS. The voice of God-Goddess within me directs me in the rightful use of energy. I will respond by compassionately acting upon this wise guidance.

My inner shepherd nurtures and protects me. I walk in green pastures beside calm waters as I diligently align my will with the will of the Christ within me. I align my emotions with the heart of the Divine Mother and I align my thoughts with the mind of the Divine Father.

I long to know myself more deeply as a living Christ. I absorb Divine Love's nurturing embrace. I allow my higher consciousness to be fully present in my human experience. I receive into my human DNA the ascension codes sown by Christ. Every cell of my body and every atom of matter is receiving the fast-vibrating (pure), ever-expanding frequencies of cosmic light, which are penetrating the Earth's atmosphere and collective consciousness of humanity. I am now able to receive a full spectrum of light; and I anchor these vibrations in the core of Mother Earth.

My desire is to expand my spiritual awareness and know union with God-Goddess while in this physical body. Thank you for teaching me how to expand my consciousness into my subtle bodies in order to activate the Christ codes within my physical body. Awaken me to receive the energies of transmutation and ascension and master the secrets of cellular regeneration. This will renew my body for eternal youth and healthful immortality. Thank you for assistance in preparing my light body and merkaba for internal and multidimensional travel.

I honor my place, part, and power in bringing heaven to earth through my thoughts, feelings, beliefs, and actions. I effect harmonious change in the world and help midwife the Earth into the next age of evolution. Thank you for helping me prepare the womb of my heart to immaculately conceive and birth the Christ Consciousness on Earth.

I submit to the process that dethrones my fear-based ego. I receive help in manifesting my desire to loosen and transmute all fear lodged in my mind, which resulted from my former beliefs in separation. I allow the necessary attunements to occur in my mind and body. I permit the transmutation of karmic patterns within my cellular memory. As I shake off old limiting thoughts and beliefs, I awaken patterns of global unity to reveal more loving ways to be in relationship with God-Goddess, myself, and others.

Like our blessed Mother Mary, I dedicate my mind, body, and soul to the Cosmic Christ being birthed on earth now. May the Divine Mother express through me Her empowering and loving presence that heals the suffering and transforms the mental and emotional fields of the world.

Open the gates that lead to the One who knows the truth beyond the Earthly deception of separation. I choose to increase in wisdom so I may be of service to others as a model of love, light, peace, and joy. Let me be a vessel that brings peace to this planet. Help me succeed in my journey through this world and know the blessings of my eternal self.

May the entire Earth and all of humanity collectively ascend during my lifetime. Help us to evolve our thinking, attuning it to the love and light of God-Goddess, so we may outwardly radiate into our world the oneness we have with Spirit. May each soul accept, feel, and become one with the energy of love as we merge with the Christ Consciousness, now arising on Earth. Let light descend upon Earth for our resurrection from the ashes of duality is nigh!

I thank my spiritual guides and all those who assist me with evolving and mastering my own soul. I am honored to be part of the process that helps to liberate the collective consciousness of Earth. I receive all the gifts the Holy Spirit wishes to impart to me. I will use these tools and abilities for the greater good of all.

Help me to abide in this Sacred Heart space of the now moment where Spirit intimately communes with me. There, I understand the roles I agreed to play before I incarnated. There, I find wisdom and strength to carry forth this plan with ease of wellbeing and lightness of heart.

All this or something better. Thank you and so it is.

Prayer for Integrating Thought Forms

The ego is a thought form or energy that exists in our 3-D experience of perceived separateness from our higher self/Source. As we restore conscious connection to our higher self in the Sacred Heart, we may have negative thoughts rising to the surface to be integrated. Here is a prayer to help integrate these energies and transmute negativity into purer thoughts:

Purify all my thought forms with brilliant, loving light. Transmute the thoughts of collective humanity with pure, loving light from the cosmic mind and heart. Let my thoughts be positive and loving at all times and in all ways. And so it is.

Prayer to Overcome Fear

Fear has to do with punishment, loss, damage, pain, sickness, illness, and darkness. In God, Who is perfect love, there is no fear.

Fear cannot coexist with unconditional love, for one repels the other. If we allow our minds to be fearful, it's like saying to the universe that we believe that something or someone has power to harm us and that God does not desire or have the ability to protect us. Do you think evil is greater than God, or that He wants to punish or rob you, or cause you pain or loss? Ego is full of fear. Thankfully, God is greater than our ego.

Bliss in Divine Oneness is an audio book set to background music that you can download at no cost when you join my mailing list. Simply click the Contact/Follow tab on my blog: http://weareoneinspirit.blogspot.com to access the sign up page. In that audio book, there is an affirming prayer with these words:

> *Only that which is of God can affect me. The peace that passes my ego's understanding cannot be shaken by errors of any kind. Peace denies the ability of anything not of God to affect me. All my thoughts have equal power. The denial of erroneous thoughts frees my mind and allows truth to guide my every thought.*

> *As a man thinks, so is he. Where my heart is, there is my treasure. My treasure is truth. My mind is filled with truth, not human perception. Not judgment or condemnation. Not separation or sin, for there are no such things in the Christ. The at-one-ment is my defense and protection. I receive this miracle now. I am healed of wrong thinking. God is greater than my fear. God is love, and love is greater than any lie I have ever believed. So be it!*

Release Prayer for Walk-ins

If you are a walk-in soul having trouble with clearing the energetic imprints left by the walk-out soul, you may find this prayer helpful. Repeat this prayer until you feel the process has been completed.

> *I call upon the Cosmic Christ Consciousness and ask for divine intervention from my spirit guides, angels, archangels, ascended masters, teachers, divine*

mother/father (whomever in spirit you trust and feel close to). I ask you to be present now.

On behalf of all the cells of my body, I ask Master St. Germain to bring the Violet Flame of Transmutation to remove and transmute all toxins, traumas, illnesses, death urges, addictions, and other detrimental residue leftover from the natal soul. I ask this to be done gently through normal elimination systems and with every breath I exhale. Let this be done only to the degree that I can energetically tolerate and without any fear. I trust there will be only positive and beneficial side effects to my physical, mental, spiritual, and emotional bodies.

Thank you for a graceful shifting out of the natal soul's personality, thoughts, emotions, cellular memories, genetic issues, soul contracts, and alignment with dark forces. In this transformation, I claim perfect health, pure thoughts, and my own mission in alignment with my soul's highest purpose and the Divine Plan.

So be it.

Praying in Spiritual Languages

My spiritual purification practices are widely varied. I may use a different tool each day of the week, or I may incorporate several techniques into one session. That's the beauty of not being tied to a religion that issues rules and regulations. Many times I arise in the morning already knowing what I need to read, chant, pray, or use as meditation tools. I invite you to follow whatever notion your heart and guidance is giving each day.

Besides conscious breathing, one technique that I employ during almost all my prayer efforts is the prayer language, which is typically received when someone is baptized in the Holy Spirit in a Pentecostal church (see 1 Corinthians 12). This gift manifested without any effort on my part when I was praying one day in 1994. I have used it ever since because I like the way it prevents my human thought processes from interfering with what my spirit (higher self) is praying. Having this tool may or may not appeal to you. As a seeker, you will find whatever you need when you need it. If you are interested in having a prayer language in your spiritual toolkit, simply ask the Holy Spirit for it. Trust that it will be imparted.

Vibrational Sound Therapy

Humans are hard-wired to respond to sound and vibration. Therefore, sound has a profound effect upon us. Much of the sounds around us—airplanes, traffic, people shouting—is uncontrollable and unpleasant. We suppress or tune out much of the noise surrounding us. We may not even be aware of how sound affects us physiologically (breathing, heartbeat, hormone levels, etc.), psychologically (emotions and feelings), cognitively (productivity, thinking processes), and behaviorally (makes you want to move, dance, or get away from unpleasant sounds). Controlled sound (the kind you create or naturally desire) can be very helpful in bringing health to the body, calming the nervous system and emotions, and stimulating brainwaves.

Chanting, Intoning, and Singing

Om. . . om. . . om. Through chanting, singing, humming, or intoning, the human voice can be used to raise the vibration of the body, mind, emotions, and soul. Om or aum is the universal sound, the song of the heart, that brings us back to oneness. Anyone can resonate this word/tone alone or in a group—even if you think you don't have a singing voice—because it doesn't matter if you match pitch with others.

Do As One (http://doasone.org) has an Om Room and I've found it a great way to add my energy to the collective consciousness as I meditate, chant om, or breathe in sync with likeminded others.

Singing Tibetan Bowls

For many years, I admired those metal bowls that "sing" by simultaneously producing two audible harmonic overtones when the rim or sides are tapped or rubbed with a mallet. I got my first bowl for my birthday last year and enjoy using it during my meditation, chanting, and prayer sessions. I also enjoy listening to CDs of singing bowls.

According to Joseph Feinstein, singing bowls were traditionally used in Asia. Making sound with bronze bowls may date back 3,000 or more years to the Bronze Age. Even though they are often referred to as Tibetan singing bowls, there are none found in the Himalayan region. Today, they are made in Nepal, India, Japan, China, and Korea.

Mind Transformation

Under the heading of mind transformation, there are a variety of techniques that can help us master the power of our own mind rather than being controlled by the negative thoughts of separation that we have created as a group mind (collective consciousness).

Subliminal Messages & Brainwave Syncing

The word "subliminal" refers to messages that bypass the thinking part of our mind and are perceived below the level of conscious awareness. Often coupled with hypnosis, soothing sounds, music, or pulsating tones (to create brainwave synchronization), subliminal recordings are recently discovered self-development tools that bring the subconscious mind into a more receptive state to help people make dramatic life changes.

I've been using brainwave entrainment audios to sync the left and right hemispheres of my brain and produce a change in behavior by modifying thinking patterns. Many of them also have subliminal messages. This tool is inexpensive and involves little effort; I've downloaded several MP3s from the Internet and listen to them with headphones (as recommended) almost every day. Sometimes I have them playing in the background while I'm working, or leave them on while I am sleeping. This can have a cathartic effect as it brings things from the subconscious to the conscious mind, so don't be surprised if you have to deal with the sludge that comes to the top to be transmuted and integrated. Process (acknowledge and clear) them. Keep your focus positive.

NeuroLinguistic Programming

Feelings accompany whatever you are thinking about. If you have a fear of something you are thinking about, it will register a response in your body. NeuroLinguisitc programming (NLP) shows you how you are communicating to yourself and helps you create new kinds of feelings regarding the way you think about certain things.

Neuro refers to the brain and the neural network, including neurons and nerve cells that send, receive, and store signals and information. **Linguistics** refers to the verbal and non-verbal messages that move through our neural pathways. **Programming** is the way the content or signal is manipulated to convert it into useful information. The words we use reflect a subconscious perception of our problems. Like a self-fulfilling prophecy, these inaccurate words and perceptions can create an underlying problem as long as we continue to think them.

NLP theory presents several ways to break learned behaviors or habits and create new ones. Therapeutic benefits include relief from anxiety, stress, phobias, or unwanted habits, or a boost to personal growth, self-development, or higher achievement (greater confidence, better focus, or improved communication skills).

Hypnosis

Like NLP, hypnosis directly accesses a person's subconscious mind, where our self-limiting beliefs are held. This powerful tool for creating positive change has gotten a bad reputation from media that depicts people walking around in zombie-like states, clucking like chickens and engaging in all kinds of ridiculous activities as commanded by the "hypno-master." While they may be open to suggestions, those in a hypnotic trance are not slaves to their masters. They are very relaxed (like how you feel just before falling asleep) and experience heightened imagination, but they are awake and have absolute free will. If you have ever been so engaged in thought while driving that you missed your exit, you have been in a hypnotic state. While in hypnosis, you may be asked to recall past lives, tell about repressed traumatic events, or reveal the reason why you fear a particular thing. Hypnotherapy can be used for gathering information and depositing positive solutions into the subconscious mind.

Working with Sacred Geometry

Sacred geometry is an ancient science that explores and explains the energy patterns that create and unify all things. It reveals the precise way that the energy of creation organizes itself. It is a catch-all term used to describe the religious, philosophical symbols, and spiritual beliefs that have evolved around geometry in various cultures throughout human history.

From the spirals in a sea shell to the proportional lines in the Star of David, symbols and patterns are found everywhere. Think of the helix of our DNA, the beauty of a snowflake or ice crystal, the repeated symmetrical points of a pine cone or flower, and the whirling of a galaxy of stars and you have examples of sacred geometry that reminds us of how intricately intelligent all of creation is. All life forms emerge out of timeless geometric codes. But nature isn't the only place you will find sacred geometry that reconnects us to sacred paths. Notice the architecture in churches, tabernacles, temples, mosques, public buildings, religious monuments, crop circles, sacred groves, and religious art.

Numbers have symbolic meanings other than their ordinary use for counting. Geometric shapes such as circles, triangles, squares, hexagons, polygons, etc. can be repeated to create coded art that represents mystical and other-world realities. Viewing and contemplating these codes offers us a glimpse into the inner workings of the universal mind and the universe itself.

Meditation

Take, take, take! Gimme, gimme, gimme! Day in and day out, your friends, family, coworkers, employers—everyone seems to demand your time and attention.

You need your energy for your own ascension. Meditation is one way you can give energy back to yourself. It has so many benefits— mentally, emotionally, spiritually, and physically—and brings calmness and brighter perspectives as it dissipates negativity. It washes away stress and enhances intuitive senses as you still your mind. It creates a channel through which divine inspiration and higher guidance can be accessed and received.

Whether alone or with a group, meditation is the art of being still to know your own power and true self. You could do a silent or verbal session (chanting, prayer, affirmations) or you might choose from a wide variety of tools to help you focus your energy and thoughts, or raise your vibration while meditating. These tools include, but are not limited to, videos, audios, drumming, conscious breathing, visualization, chanting, singing, praying, laying in trance or altered states, and repeating mantras or affirmations. Taking time out of the mundane, helps relieve stress and connect you with the Sacred Heart within.

Meditation is a great time to daydream and use your imagination to create by visualizing what you want. It helps to set an intention for the meditation. Many times I try to envision what our society would look like if we all laid down our weapons of war and critical judgment and simply accepted what is. It is a beautiful vision. You are free to create your own vision of utopia.

If you are in the Nashville area, you may enjoy participating in a Sacred Circle that my friend, Vickie B. Majors, initiated to support the ascension process and bring world peace. Contact me if you would like more information about this group.

Communing with Nature

Being in nature is such a great way to feel grounded and centered! You unknowingly interact with the elementals, which are light beings in a dimension unseen by most human eyes. Air, fire, water, and earth are the elements of our human birth. Breathing fresh air, feeling the heat of the sun, walking near (or getting into) water, or touching the soil is refreshing to the body and spirit. As you walk in nature, incorporate life-giving breath by breathing in for six steps and breathing out for six steps. The act of walking calls forth the energy or prana from Earth's etheric body into yours. This is one of the reasons why you feel so refreshed and recharged by the end of a nature walk.

If you feel weak, sick, frustrated, angry, or find yourself dealing with any ascension disturbances (the mud being stirred up), the last thing you may want to do is get outdoors—especially if the weather is unpleasant. During the times I have forced myself to get outside and enjoy nature (even if only for a few minutes), I notice my attitude starts to change. If it's raining or cold and you simply can't seem to motivate yourself to go outdoors, find a sunny window and soak in the rays of the sun indoors.

Exercise

While I'm not an advocate of high-impact exercise, I know we "gotta move it, move it" to keep the energy flowing and the physical body strong. I prefer low-impact ones like yoga, swimming, or walking in nature because these forms of movement allow us to reconnect to nature and the elements. If the weather is less than ideal, I can work up a sweat by dancing without pounding my feet into my knees or looking like a klutz who can't get coordinated with the rest of the class. To each her own. Just get your body in motion.

When I was having problems with fibromyalgia shortly after my 1999 walk-in experience, my doctor recommended daily exercise. I was living in an apartment complex that had an indoor swimming pool. There were days when I didn't even feel like walking to the pool, much less exerting the effort to swim laps. On the days that I did swim, I found it helped ease the pain and put me in a better frame of mind.

It wasn't until I discovered yoga and conscious breathing that I started truly seeing the benefit that movement and breath has upon a weary body. Yoga is a non-impact form of cardio-vascular exercise that tones the muscles while increasing flexibility. Because the poses can be adapted to your current level of physical ability, almost anyone can enjoy practicing yoga. Because it uses the breath to calm the mind and body, it is a spiritual practice that has benefited devotees for centuries. There are numerous books, videos, and even iPhone apps that make it convenient to do yoga at home.

Cleansing the Body

You don't have to look very far to see how bad we have polluted the water, soil, and air of our environment. We have buried toxic waste in the ground and dumped rubbish in the oceans. Of course, this detrimentally affects all species. You might be surprised, however, that the most damage we do to our bodies is through what we eat and drink. In ascension, the physical body is constantly detoxifying and constructing the light body. Adding contaminants to what needs to be detoxified, slows down the entire process of ascension. Gradually over many years in the ascension process, new frequencies will dissolve and transmute these toxins along with the thought form of separation. Once this occurs, disease and decay will cease to be experienced. Until then, we can do ourselves a big favor and begin our reconnection to the Earth by refusing to eat processed foods and begin eating a plant-based diet—one that is primarily vegetables, grains, legumes, nuts, and fruits that contain chi or life-force energy. The fresher the food, the more chi it provides. Like Hippocrates said, "Let your food be your medicine, your medicine be your food." If you take care of yourself, you'll be better prepared for the shift.

You can also support the body in the ascension process by doing a cleanse that flushes impurities from the system. There are numerous dietary programs that help clean the colon, gallbladder, liver, kidneys, and digestive system. If your body is feeling lethargic, you might research your options and intuitively discern which type of cleanse is best for you. Fasting from food—even if only for one meal—is one way to cleanse the body and let the digestive tract rest. Fasting can also serve a spiritual purpose if your intention is set to do so. When changing your diet or beginning the practice of fasting, it's best to change things gradually and see how your body responds. During the writing of this book, I felt motivated and gained the wisdom to become a vegetarian. It has made a tremendous difference not only in the way I feel physically, but in the peace and clarity of mind that I enjoy to a greater degree than ever.

Baths and Salt Scrubs

The skin is the largest organ of the body. It not only protects everything inside our body, it brings in energy from our environment. Removing dead skin cells once or twice a week helps rejuvenate the skin, making it more efficient in detoxifying. It also brings new life to your complexion. Since there are different types of skin on your body, you wouldn't use the same exfoliant all over. The larger granules of salt (or sugar) are great for the feet, while the tiny, mildly-abrasive particles in baking soda are great for the face.

A bath in Epsom salt, baking soda, and sea salt can help draw out impurities in the skin, reduce soreness in muscles, and clear the field around the body. There are many essential oils that can be added to your bath. My favorites are lavender and bergamot. You can create your own mixture by adding essential oils to a cup of salt and half-cup of almond or olive oil. Mix well and then use it as a scrub or pour it into the bath water.

Receiving Energy Work

Reiki, reconnective healing, acupuncture/acupressure, EFT, healing touch, quantum angel healing, shamanic healing. . . the list goes on. There are many modalities that can help to clear old patterns, open the chakras, subtle bodies, mind, and cells of the body. If you feel that your present condition is more than you can handle alone, I encourage you to seek a practitioner who can help you clear your field and process the underlying emotions that are causing your discomfort.

Being Fully Present in Your Body

In order to fully feel your feelings, you must be fully present in your body; not floating around up in the ethers, but fully integrated, with your feet planted firmly on the Earth. This is where grounding and centering comes in. If you are not present in your body, it is not possible to fully feel your feelings and process them. Listen to what your body and emotions are telling you. If they are negative or uncomfortable, consider what thoughts or beliefs they are pointing to that need changing or realigning. I don't think it is necessary to figure out what happened in a past life unless you truly feel this is the root to what's causing your current dilemma. In those cases, a past-life regression might bring understanding to help you process what you need to do next. It's best to simply accept what is happening now. Focus on this moment or where you want to be rather than on where you have been.

That's not to say that you shouldn't express your feelings. I certainly am not suggesting that you deny, repress, or judge them. What I mean is it's not necessary to wallow in guilt, despair, and shame, or give undesirable emotions undue attention. For example, if you start feeling sorry for yourself, you can nip self-pity in the bud. If I experience something upsetting with another person, I've found it effective to write a letter (and then burn it without giving it to the person), or pretend that the offender is sitting in front of me while I calmly speak my truth. Voicing your concerns privately in this manner releases the internal pressure of unexpressed e-motions—energy in motion. I have seen issues resolved by calling a spirit-to-spirit meeting with my guides and the guides of the person I am upset with. I like to end these sessions by offering forgiveness, which moves the ego out of the way and allows divine light to do what it does best—heal our bodies, situations, the collective mind, and the planet from the illusion of separation.

Venting without self-control (spirit control!) can be embarrassing or dangerous as it riles the ego in both parties and only makes the situation worse. If you can sit down calmly with the other person and discuss the situation in a non-accusing manner and without allowing your emotions to get in the way, that's great! Your thoughts are becoming purer and more loving.

Sending Light to Others

There's a lot of talk about light these days. Many people, including me, sign their emails with something like "Love and Light." How does that effort benefit anyone? The light represents oneness or unity with God-Goddess, which brings peace of mind as it purifies our thoughts and allows higher truth to guide us. Light is the resolution of all conflicts and thoughts propagated by the ego's belief in separation. Light is a pure state of mind that is so unified with Source that darkness cannot be perceived in another person. Therefore, light makes it possible to see as God-Goddess sees.

You cannot find light by analyzing darkness. As Saint Germain revealed to Godfré Ray King in *Unveiled Mysteries*, "No one can keep his thoughts and feelings qualified with Perfection unless he goes to the 'Source of Perfection,' for that quality and activity only abide within the God Flame." Light is within us. It is our Divine nature. There is chaos and darkness all around us. We are to mindfully choose our response to each thought or feeling that comes our way. As the old saying goes, "A bird may land on your head, but you don't have to let it build a nest there." Saying "no" to discordant energy and saying "yes" to the Light of God-Goddess within your heart is the correct way to use energy. The kingdom of God is right mindedness (right use of energy), peace, and joy. If anything manifests as something other than this loving nature it is not your true self. It is the ego's device to keep you from recognizing your oneness with the divine. To rise above the veil that causes us to see ourselves as something other than a perfect child of God, we must allow the light to shine through us and upon us.

By acknowledging darkness through harboring fear, hatred, resentment, and judgment, we allow it to grow. That's because what we focus on increases. Focus on the light and love within yourself and others; it will grow and transform your mind, reprogramming it to think on higher things. This is your true nature/self—your spiritual essence that has been hidden by the illusion of fear. Perceive light in yourself and others to experience a miraculous return to wholeness.

Imagine you are in a tent, camping out in your own backyard. When you turn on a flashlight you can see everything inside the tent. The darkness is still outside your tent. Now you turn on the floodlights in your yard, and the area around you contains less darkness. At sunrise, there is even more light around you. At mid-day there is no darkness at all. Compare this to your own spiritual light. There is enough light inside you (your own tent) to light your own path. When you expand your light into your aura, it's like turning on the floodlights in your backyard. You begin to affect others with your light. Once you make it clear that you want the light and that you don't want darkness around you, the universe will respond by bringing more and more light. The next thing you know, there is no darkness around you.

Grounding and Centering

With so many accelerated frequencies from the cosmos permeating the Earth's atmosphere, you may find that you become ungrounded more easily these days. Therefore, grounding is more important now to your emotional and energetic well-being than ever before. Grounding your energy brings you fully present in your body. Compared to a three-pronged electric cord, your grounding cord neutralizes the surge of accelerated frequencies your body picks up and doesn't know what to do with. The Earth energies that you bring upward into your body during the grounding process help stabilize cosmic energies in your body and on the Earth. Grounding also protects your nervous system from the "shock" that comes from having too much fast-vibrating energy in the body. This is the nervousness, anxiety, confusion, and brain fog many people feel after having a spiritually-transforming experience.

Grounding can be accomplished in a variety of ways. You can visualize your roots growing down into the Earth. You can get outside in nature—it's especially helpful to walk barefoot on the ground. Eating, doing physical exercise, or breathing consciously can help center you in your body.

Before you begin this exercise, you need to choose a color for your grounding cord. Try on different ones until you find one that feels right and aligns with whatever you need that day.

Part One:

- I see divine white light clearing my body and aura as it enters the crown of my head from the cosmos. This cleansing, loving light flows through me and exits my feet where it goes into the Earth and the very center of Mother Gaia.

- The grounding cord extending from my body is _____ (color).

- My aura extends 2.5 feet from my body.

- I see a sparkling shower of golden sunlight washing my aura. Archangels Michael and Chamuel are in place to help with this process.

- Christ-gold light surrounds me. Certainty blue light surrounds me.

- The Violet flame of St. Germain is in place outside my aura to absorb any detrimental energy released in this session and transmute it into beneficial energy for me, my life, my body, and others.

Part Two:

- Cosmic gold light energy begins in my crown, flows down my spine and the back of my chakras, and curves under my tail bone. Ten percent flows down through my grounding cord. The other 90 percent flows upward to my fifth chakra where it divides three ways: upward and out through my crown, down each shoulder and arm, and then out the palms.

- Mother Gaia's love and light Earth energies ascend through my feet, up my legs, joining with the cosmic gold flow at my tail bone and flowing consecutively with the cosmic gold light for the next ten minutes.

Should Drugs Be Used to Help with Integration?

In addition to having a family history of depression, my walk-in experience brought a sudden download of higher energy into my physical body. According to one psychic reading I got in the early 2000s, this "fried" my nervous system and created a chemical imbalance in my brain, causing confusion, fogginess, and a heightened sensitivity to energy and environmental stimuli. Since I was burned out and had a very strong tendency toward suicide at the time, my doctor prescribed an anti-depressant that most likely saved my life. Therefore, I will never tell someone not to take a medication that benefits their overall well-being. However, it would have been much better to have been treated with natural supplements and phytotherapy rather than synthetic drugs. These plant-based remedies weren't readily available when I needed them more than a decade ago, but they are now. The strength or potency level needed to effectively treat many conditions is much higher than what you can get in herbal supplements purchased over the counter. Rather than self-treating, you are better off to consult a medical doctor known as a naturopathic physician, who uses phytotherapy and high-quality supplements to treat root causes.

Being on a drug or herbal supplement that eases symptoms doesn't excuse anyone from practicing spiritual purification. The anti-depressant helped me manage symptoms of empathy fatigue while I worked diligently to heal my body and clear unresolved karma left by the natal soul. During the decade that I took the medication, I continuously looked forward to the day that I would be able to manage without it. That day finally came once I learned how to manage energy as an empath. I am now free of all prescription medications.

When I was suffering with depression, I had a friend who chided me because I was taking a medication to help balance the chemcial levels in my brain so my body could function better and with less stress. She believed that only "natural" (drug-free) healing was of God and she discredited and frowned upon any dependence upon a drug to rebalance the human body. No one should force you to adhere to their particular belief about anything! You and your divine guidance know what is right for your body and your spiritual path. God gives us all things freely to enjoy. So, whether it is allopathic medicine, surgery, physical therapy, diet, exercise, vitamins/supplements, flower essence, meditation, energy work, aromatherapy, some ancient modality, or the suggestions in this book, everything we do to help our bodies integrate these purer frequencies is welcome to participate in the routine for staying healthy.

Be sure to seek the gift in whatever discomfort your body is manifesting. Pain is your body's way of communicating with you that something that is out of alignment. Ask yourself, your body, and your guides what the underlying message or belief is that needs to shift. Then, take action upon what you discern. If you need to forgive someone (even yourself), do that. If you need to stop being around a particular person or situation, set and maintain stronger boundaries. If you need medical treatment, get it. If you feel a massage would help, call for an appointment. If you need energetic healing or prayer, ask someone you trust to pray for you or send love and light.

In holistic treatment there is no "us" and "them," right or wrong, good or bad. All components can be integrated, and all things can work together for good. Your body is yours to manage. Do whatever you think is best for it, and know that you are always loved!

Chapter 6 ~ Hindrances to Integration

The ego is one of the main things we have to deal with when
ascending or having a more evolved soul or higher vibration enter
the body. Purer frequencies automatically start clearing out dark
energy in an attempt to align the soul with pure consciousness.
Think of entrainment. When there are two vibrations—one high
and one low—in close proximity, either the low vibration one will
be raised, the high vibration will be lowered, or they will meet in
the middle. The same is true about resonation. If you pluck the E
string on one guitar in a quiet room, soon all the E strings on the
other guitars in the room will start to vibrate. This is similar to what
is happening to humanity. The Earth is raising her vibrational pitch
and we are changing and raising our vibration to align with it. We
can no longer ignore what is going on around us. We do ourselves a
favor by cooperating and letting go of whatever is not in alignment
with this new frequency.

There are some behaviors
that interfere with this
process and actually create
detrimental energy and

> Judge not that ye be not judged.
>
> ~ Matthew 7:1

strengthen the ego's vices and humanity's perception of
separation. For example, revengeful thoughts create revengeful
behavior like war, violence, and fighting. Kind thoughts create
considerate and respectful behavior. Jealous thoughts create

jealous and defensive behavior. Peaceful thoughts create peaceful behavior. In other words, our thoughts create our behavior, and our behavior creates our reality in life. It makes sense then to monitor what we are thinking and change our thoughts whenever they are not pure.

When Jesus was quoted as saying "Judge not that ye be not judged," I think the interpretation is that we should examine ourselves and our motives before we try to correct someone else. I don't know about you, but I find it a full time job to "catch and clear" my own mental and emotional stuff without meddling in someone else's business.

Judging others or yourself lowers your energy and vibration. Most of the time we don't know enough about a person or situation before we form an opinion or issue a judgment. The thing we judge in someone else may be the very thing we are secretly guilty of. If you're pointing a finger at someone else, remember to look inside to see why this person's behavior is pushing your buttons. The more you love and respect yourself, the less you will judge others or be affected by the judgments of others. Self-love frees you to walk your own path and allow others to walk theirs.

There is no sin; hence, we are sinless. Some readers may have a hard time grasping the fact that there is no good and evil, right or wrong, but if you believe that Christ paid for your sins, then how is that different from the idea that there is no sin? Unless we throw out the Bible and dismiss it entirely, we must admit that the major theme in Jesus' teaching is acceptance and inclusion. "Forgive everyone" is the same as saying, "if you cannot accept the idea that there is no sin, forgive everyone of whatever you *think* or *claim to be* sin." Pure thoughts exist where there is no criticism or judgment—in other words where the ego has no rule. If only we could see that the divine exists within us and that we are individuations of God-Goddess. How much better would we treat ourselves, others, animals, the environment, and all of creation?

"The idea that within each of us is the god we seek is so contrary to what we have been conditioned to believe that the mention of it is to blaspheme against the finite god we think we know and believe in," writes Carl Bozeman. "Our reasoning protects us from the awesome power and responsibility of being god, accepting our divine nature, and seeing beyond the reality we have come to know. "

Carl's book, *On Being God*, is filled with some of the most profound statements and insights of any book I have read regarding the limitations we humans place upon ourselves. Carl's interpretation of the story of the Garden of Eden makes much better sense than the one advocated in traditional Christian teachings. Carl proposes that the alleged serpent is actually our ego, which deceives us with endless mind chatter that keeps us from knowing we are gods. We are so much greater than we have realized. We are individuations, sparks of the divine source, having limitless possibility to create anything. There was no serpent beguiling Eve. Her own thinking deceived her and she shared with Adam her conclusion that we are something other than God. As a society we have created our own image of god. We then limit that entity as we have limited ourselves with our ego—the small-self thinking that feels a sense of entitlement at the expense of excluding or violating others.

Abuse and the Victim Mentality

The ego does everything it can to slow down your integration and ascension process. Victim mindset and judgmental attitudes are two of the biggest hindrances. One huge step in clearing your energy field and beginning to create purer frequencies is to stop seeing yourself as a victim—of anything! We create our own circumstances through choices we have made either at a soul level (which may seem involuntary on the physical plane), on purpose, or by default (doing nothing to actively pursue a better outcome). Abuse is not something any of us consciously want to manifest, but you are only a victim if you choose to see yourself that way. You can change your perception about an abusive experience and thereby change your future, healing your emotions in the process.

Harboring resentment, attempting to retaliate, seeing yourself as a victim, and blaming others are signs of a cluttered energy field. And, these things provide a nice incubator for detrimental energy. Remember, energy attracts more energy like itself. Empaths can't keep from sensing energy—it's part of our reason for being in body—but we *can* keep from absorbing it and allowing it to drag us down or make us sick. That's why it is necessary forgive.

Let's talk about three reasons from an empowered soul perspective as to why abuse occurs.

Soul Development

One way to overcome abuse is to accept it as part of your soul's development plan. The act of abuse could have been arranged by your soul with another soul to help you discover a particular strength or virtue, or to allow you to become a mentor to new souls who are suffering abuse now. One who has overcome the hardship of abuse and is now living a victorious life is a good example to those who need to see their own potential.

Karma and Repaying Debts

I've heard people say that abuse occurs as a result of karmic debts being repaid. Personally, I don't believe in karma—it's a retribution mindset and is not part of pure consciousness. We live in an age of grace, but we do have free will. Therefore, two souls in an abusive relationship may connect in the afterlife and continue their ego battle while stuck in the Earth plane. Then these earthbound souls reincarnate into close proximity to one another where they may continue this abusive behavior while in physical body. This could be a cycle that some souls perpetuate, but according to *The Spirit's Book*, a channeled work by Allan Kardec, this behavior will eventually cease as these souls decide they've had enough, and finally cross over into the light, develop their souls, and begin to vibrate at a purer frequency.

Nothing negative that happens on this Earth plane needs to go with us into the afterlife. We take our lessons with us when we cross into the light. It is the souls who do not cross over (earthbound souls) that continue to experience the mental and emotional suffering they endured while in body. You can stop this cycle now by refusing to see yourself as a victim and no longer engaging in retaliating behavior.

Shirking Responsibility

An act of violence could happen because some soul who agreed to protect you did not step in. That soul may have gotten trapped in a codependent relationship that didn't allow them to learn the lesson they were supposed to in order to shield you. In this case, you could blame the other soul for allowing the abuse to happen, but doing so will only permit you to continue to see yourself as a victim; and it will delay your healing and keep you from taking the next step toward empowerment.

Our egos will find any excuse to avoid taking responsibility for where we are now and what we have created with our negative thoughts. Regardless of what has happened in your past you are the only one who can make the decision to let go of offenses and get on with your life's purpose. The longer you hang on to the victim mentality, the more you will continue to attract abuse and detrimental energy into your life experience.

You will never be able to fulfill your divine mission for being here if you stay stuck licking your wounds. Do whatever you need to do to heal, forgive, and move forward. Remember that whatever you focus on or think about comes about. Focusing on past abuse is the same as currently abusing yourself! You may not have physical scars, but in essence you are picking the crust off of emotional wounds that are trying to heal. Focus on the light and love within you. Be good to yourself. Forgive everything that has happened to you in the past and allow your higher guidance to assist you in realizing that you are an empowered being now.

What are Lower Vibrating Energies?

First of all, let me state that there is no "good" or "bad" energy. We put those labels on things using our human judgment of what we perceive to be pleasant or unpleasant. The labels are not important. The fact remains that we are being called to awaken to our authentic spiritual selves. All this impure stuff is not us—it's not who we really are as sparks of divine light. This combative energy resides in denser planes of consciousness as part of "all possibilities." Without having a choice about what we do, think, say, or feel, we are puppets without free will. Other options must exist, but if they bring us displeasure, we can avoid attracting them in to our lives. Like weeds among edible plants in a garden, they exist together.

There are two sides to everything: dark/light, yin/yang, positive/negative, and so on. In order for peace to prevail these opposites need to be in balance. Presently, we have more masculine (aggressive) energy on the planet than feminine (passive) energy. This imbalance is being corrected by the cosmos.

We often yield our divine nature to the irrational reasoning of the ego. I believe the ego is what many religions refer to as the anti-Christ. The ego opposes everything the Christ consciousness stands for and urges us to create sorrow, suffering, and violence in this world. Negative or dark energy has a direct association to our ego. We may call it by many names—the devil, Satan, demons, evil, the fall, fallen angels, entities, disincarnate souls, earthbound spirits. I dislike the connotation these terms evoke, but it all boils down to a thought form that perpetuates the belief in separation from God or the pure Divine essence of ALL THAT IS. The word "entity" implies that something has a self-contained existence in either material or non-material form. Regardless of whether this thought form has an actual identity, or if they are real or imagined, the trouble they cause us must be dealt with during the ascension process. Since most people believe angels are positive messengers of the light, let's suppose for a moment that negative energy also contains entities that carry messages.

Entities and Earthbound Spirits

Disincarnate spirits (souls who have been in a body) can exert a subtle or direct influence—both good and bad—upon humans. They may influence us without our awareness by offering inspiration that we express through writing, speaking, and other creative or artistic ventures. Or they may tempt us to do something harmful to a living creature or distract us from doing something that we know is in our best interest.

It is easy to distinguish between more evolved and less advanced spirits. The language of more evolved spirits is honorable and free of bias; these may be our spirit guides. Lesser evolved spirits may use harsh language and urge us to react to situations through our ego rather than responding through the mind/heart of God-Goddess. The ego believes in the need to suffer, feel guilty, judge self and others, and do whatever it takes to defend its position.

There are more humans inhabiting the planet than ever. That means there are a higher number of entities on the Earth plane as well. Author Ethan Vorly shares that entities are the unresolved karma or crystallization that was housed in the astral body of someone who has died and was not cremated. We know that fire and smoke are purifying agents, and this is probably why many ancient cultures performed last rites for a departing soul and burned the physical body on a funeral pyre. This is said to dismantle the astral body and transmute its negative karma. If this is true, then it certainly explains why we have seen such a huge increase in violence, depression, and suicide since embalming and burial became the preferred method of disposing of a physical body upon death.

The energetic pattern that was attached to the astral body of a human host during an incarnation is shed like a snake skin when that host dies. As the soul ascends into higher planes and crosses into the light, the astral body is left behind to roam the Earth plane where it seeks a new host with a similar frequency. During the ascension, people are suddenly becoming more able to see, feel, hear, sense, and even smell the presence of earth-bound spirits. I've dealt with earthbound spirits on many occasions. Jesus confronted them as well; if someone asked Him to remove the "demon" (as they were called in the Bible), He obliged.

Earthbound spirits feed off the energy of humans in order to remain active. They target humans who have similar fixations as their own. It might be someone with a drug or alcohol abuse problem, someone with emotional distress in their life, trauma, abuse, or someone who is simply ungrounded or not fully participating in their own spiritual development. So when an earthbound spirit finds a human in a state of despair, having weak or no boundaries, the earthbound spirit may attach itself to that person's electromagnetic energy field that surrounds the body and is sometimes referred to as the aura. Not only does the entity start siphoning energy from the host, the negative energy of the entity contaminates the aura, causing the human host to feel out of sorts, have dysfunctional thoughts, feel physically sick, experience rampant emotions, or have cravings that are not their own. The videos at http://www.spiritistvideos.com explain the Spiritist view of entities. You may find them interesting and informative.

The best way to keep entities away is to raise your personal vibration through spiritual purification practices. Keeping your thoughts pure requires a constant effort, but as you vibrate at a purer level, these entities are less apt to bother you. It also helps to keep your aura close to your body and remove any negative or stuck energy so that these entities are no longer attracted to you. Keep focusing on the light within you, using affirmations, mantras, and clearing exercises such as smudging with sage. If things are really bad or an entity has been attached to your home or auric field for some time, you might want to use the alcohol and Epsom salt recipe mentioned in Chapter 5.

As you start to clear your field and remove layers of unresolved karma (anything not aligned with the law of grace), things can seem worse rather than better for a short while. I urge you to persevere and not quit in the process. For example, once you have cleared (or while clearing) a negative mental pattern, you may expose a dark entity, which was feeding on the energy surrounding a misaligned thought pattern. The issue brought to the light removed the entity's energy source, which can feel unsettling for the host and the entity. Since at some time in your past you gave the entity permission (most likely you were unaware of doing so) to stay and influence you, you are the one who needs to dismiss it from its duties and help it move on.

Dr. Caron Goode says that when she did past life regression, hypnosis, and light-trance sessions, she always asked the client, "Why did you create or attract this entity?" Rather than trying to "drive out demons" you may simply need to thank the entity for the purpose it served and send it into the light. However, to get an entity to go into the light, it must first realize that there is a light to go into and that it will be a pleasant experience—many do not want to go there for fear of punishment.

Remember, earthbound souls are former humans now without bodies. The reason souls become earthbound is due to their emotional problems, and just like humans in a body, they need healing. Remain non-resistant by offering compassion to these lost souls. They need the same love and light we do. They don't respond well to techniques that attempt to remove them by force. In fact, this can make things worse because even if the entity leaves, it may only be temporary, and when it returns it may be angry and seeking revenge.

The reason many clearings fail is because the person doing the clearing does not open the entity to its deeper subconscious feelings. Entities need to recognize and heal their deeper emotional scars. Free them from their misery by helping them see the role they are playing in the lives of embodied souls. Ethan Vorly writes: "Once the entity feels these deeper underlying emotions, it automatically allows the light in, which quickly transforms it. They are always sorry for what they have done and become loving beings as they are absorbed into the light where they are freed from all pain. It is truly beautiful to witness." Once the entity is ready to move on, you can use the Entity Release Prayer in the previous chapter to send it on its merry way.

In late September and early October 2011, my mind was a mess and it felt like I was not in control of the thoughts my mind was thinking. I had started nit-picking and causing arguments with my husband due to the judgmental, angry thoughts I was having about him. I also kept hearing negative thoughts like *"You aren't ascending. Who do you think you are? You shouldn't even be writing a book about the topic."*

Truth is, I didn't feel like I was ascending at all! I felt like I had deceived myself about all this spiritual purification work. It seemed I was regressing instead of ascending. Entities try to distract us by having us over-analyze what we see and hear of a negative or detrimental nature. I knew these were not my thoughts; so I took action, only to find that my clearing exercises did not work. Calling upon my guides seemed futile as if no one was listening. Smudging myself and home with sage did not clear the horrible thoughts in my head. In addition to this mental attack, my body manifested symptoms of a head cold, which challenged my ability to remain focused on my newly-forming mindset regarding immortality. I know that thoughts affect physical health, so I tried to integrate the negative energy using Tom Goode's four-step process. Remembering Tom's advice about non-resistance, I somehow managed to refrain from speaking negatively to my body or being angry that it had a condition to deal with.

While all this was occurring, I was giving out a lot of energy through my teaching and it really felt like I was being tested to find out whether or not I really believed the message I was presenting. I recorded a Halloween special with Ranoli and Caron on how to clear detrimental energy/entities. It was also the final week of "Empaths Shifting into 2012" [http://weare1inspirit.com/spiritual-audios.htm#All8]. I find it humorous now that my topic was on how we are not victims of anything and that we create our own reality with our thoughts.

I retraced the beginning of this mental bombardment and realized I had picked up this negative energy pattern at the liquor store almost two weeks prior, when I decided that a bottle of red wine might go well with dinner. As I got out of the car that Friday afternoon I heard, "Ground and center. Put your shields up." I foolishly ignored this advice from my higher guidance and went inside. I was only in there for about three minutes but trouble followed me home. I should have suspected an earthbound soul was at work when my husband saw a vapor pass between us while we were watching TV that night.

I was vulnerable when I went into the liquor store that day because I had been releasing some mental patterns regarding an abuse that had happened in my childhood—an issue I had cleared years ago. I now realize that this issue belonged to Bon (the natal soul of this body). Now that her energy was merged with mine, she had a few more things to integrate and heal regarding this abuse in which she had felt she was a victim. I had also been fasting to break strongholds; and I had been doing deep breathing to dismantle any hardened thought patterns in my astral and mental bodies in order to allow my Christ Self to shine through more clearly.

Needless to say, this was having a cathartic effect and I had stirred up quite a bit of emotional dirt. I was making good progress in washing it from my body by drinking a lot of water. This "psychic dust" had a frequency that resonated with the entity in the liquor store. I was, after all, not in neutral territory! Disincarnates love the energy of drugs and alcohol and tend to hang around the people who are addicted to mind-altering substances.

I decided to talk to my husband about what was going on in my head. He knows I am very energy sensitive and he has helped me deal with things like this before. Noticing a huge and negative change in me, he was more than ready to help me discover what was causing this disturbance. We both knew it was entity contamination.

As we were standing at the kitchen counter and pondering what we needed to do, Randy said, "You are a lot closer to ascending than you think." Those words broke the power that this "thing" had in my mind. I suddenly began groaning like I used to do as an intercessor. I could hardly catch a breath as all the muscles of my body began involuntarily contracting. It felt like someone was wringing liquid out of a dishcloth and I was the dishcloth! I held tightly to the granite countertop as tears started rolling down my face. As suddenly as this episode began, it all stopped. Relieved and grateful that my muscles had relaxed, I laid the upper half of my body on the cool granite surface to rest from the ordeal. My mind was silent and I felt a calmness and peace wash over my entire being. I felt the presence of angels and archangels around me.

Had I listened to my inner guidance that day at the liquor store and taken a moment to ground and center with pink light, I could have avoided this situation. However, I would not have gained the lesson I needed, nor would I have been able to compassionately release that non-physical being so it could cross over into the light and not harm anyone else. And, I would not be able to share the knowledge I am offering now. After all, what purpose does any experience serve if we can't learn from it and use it to help others avoid misery?

Coaching is a life-changing experience that allows you to quickly make spiritual changes that improve every aspect of your life. I am available to help walk-ins and empaths acclimate to the Earth plane and move into action regarding the reason they came here. If you would like to do some coaching with me, please contact me on my Website, http://weare1inspirit.com.

Chapter 7 ~ The End of Judgment

Many see the Earth as a battleground upon which the sons of light/good and the sons of darkness/evil wage war. The battle actually lies in the belief in duality or separation (ego), which is waged within every mind. Love lies at the heart of all that we seek, and separation from love is the root of our trouble and pain. It's all in how you look at the situation. God-Goddess created all things perfect and good and eternal. When we see ourselves as something *other than* a perfect creation of God, and part of the same substance as the cosmic intelligence that gave us life, we limit what we can accomplish on Earth. If we believe ourselves to be separate from Source, we will live a life that is limited in all aspects. Thinking that you are deprived of or inferior to the glory of God-Goddess will also slow down your purification process.

Because you are already part of the Christ Consciousness, union in God-Goddess can be realized in this now moment. This truth can be accessed by going within yourself to the Sacred Heart found in the now moment and allowing the Divine to express through you. You are loved totally and unconditionally by the source of creation. Opening to this love will help you experience more of your true worth, and heal the pain of separation. When you choose to be awake, aware, and appreciative of all your experiences, life will become easier. Coming to believe that you are already enlightened and ascended is greatly assisted by prayer, meditation, and spiritual purification practices.

I urge you to employ grounding and centering exercises. This daily renewing of your mind and clearing of your chakras and subtle bodies will help you to conquer your innermost fears and learn to unconditionally love yourself and others. When you see your fears for what they are and master your own thoughts and emotions, you will tap into your own spiritual power and create the life you truly want.

Practicing the techniques in this book will help you stay centered, raise the vibration of your body and mental thoughts, become a solid container for your emotions, and manage energy wisely. Ascension is not a destination at the end of a path in the distant future; it is a process we are all going through. A lot more than the prophesied 144,000 are participating in the ascension. If this book and the concepts presented here appeal to you, then you are most likely one of them.

Unfortunately, some people will refuse to change their minds or believe differently, even when they know that what they currently hold as truth is detrimentally affecting them. That is the working of the ego at its self-protective core. The ego knows that anything we ascribe to God-Goddess, we have within ourselves. In order to

> You can empower yourself to live in the moment by controlling your thoughts and emotions, and guiding yourself the way that you want to be guided, rather than allowing modern society to tell you how to feel and what to think. Just as you create your own reality, we are also co-creating our realities together. We are a collective! As a community, a city, a country, and a species, we decide where we want to go and how we want to flow. It is up to us to decide what happens next in the epic tale that is the human race, but change has to start from an individual level.
>
> ~ Spirit Science 1 - Thoughts (Revised)

realize our divine nature, we must overcome our need to judge others. The more we get rid of judgment, the more of God-Goddess we will see in ourselves. Naturally, in order to continue its own existence, the ego will show us creative ways to keep judgment alive. But it's ultimately our choice how we respond to each situation. Regardless of our religious traditions, we can appreciate and honor one another. Reverence every soul's path of evolution, ascension has little to do with religion—one path is not better than another; it has everything to do with changing one's fear-based perceptions and behaviors into a more loving and accepting way of life.

All lightworkers are helping to usher in the New Heaven and New Earth that has been prophesied, but it means that everything that can be shaken is being shaken within each of us. It is part of the ascension process and there's no need to resist it. Forgiveness of self and others is the mind-body-soul detoxification that brings purer thoughts. It liberates you from contaminated emotions and sets you free from draining attachments and dark entities. Oneness can exist in a world of duality. Eve (the feminine expression of God-Goddess—was created from Adam's rib while he was in a state of oneness where only the male expression of God-Goddess was experienced. After Eve was created, she and Adam existed together in duality (yin/yang) and there was balance, harmony, and peace. Before they acknowledged their separation from oneness, feelings of guilt, shame, greed, or need were not part of their lives.

> As you and Mother Earth are being impregnated with light, you are serving the great work of spiritualizing matter, which assists humanity's ignorant, warlike resistance to unity and harmony to shift. As this occurs, the earth plane can hold more and more coherent higher dimensional patterns of unity or Christ consciousness as you harmonize the accompanying chaotic birth pangs.
>
> ~ Claire Heartsong *Anna, Grandmother of Jesus*

Self-forgiveness dispels guilt, shame and feelings of inferiority can block your path to knowing oneness. There may be some people you choose to love from a distance, but that choice is healing nonetheless. The more you love our Creator, yourself, and others, the happier, brighter, and more successful your life will become.

The answer then is to love God-Goddess with all your heart, mind, and soul. This raises the vibration of your physical body into a higher octave or level of frequency.

Ascension comes after the resurrection from separation, but there can be no resurrection until something dies or ceases to exist. This is why many individuals are encountering a dark night of the soul and there is so much upheaval in society. The purification path to ascension has been difficult because we have resisted the process that brings an end to human suffering and dethrones the ego.

If you feel there is something in your life that needs to undergo the cleansing, refining process, be willing to allow it. Let yourself feel what you feel in order to deal with the core issue. When you deal, you will heal. As you heal yourself, you heal others and the planet. Then, the only thing left of a past belief or situation is the lesson learned—there's no emotional attachment to it. The karma (the law of sin and death) is erased from the Book of Life (Akashic Records) and the event no longer has power over you.

There is no condemnation in the Christ Consciousness. So, take responsibility for where you are now, realizing that you are a powerful co-creator as you align with the purer thoughts and frequencies of the universe. The universe has unconditional love, abundant gifts, wise guidance, and unlimited blessings for you.

You can choose to be free, regardless of what has transpired in your life, or what anyone has said to you or about you. It's simple because loving God-Goddess is about being and not doing. Spending five minutes a day in the Sacred Heart space will begin to transform you. Do the exercises in this book as a supplement, but only do them because you want to experience divine love—not because you are trying to make your light body appear. Five minutes per day in this blissful place will naturally create a desire for more divine love. You could begin to take five-minute breaks throughout the day and come into this place of calmness. Then, you could add a couple more sessions and divide your day into thirds with heart-centered meditations in the morning, after work, and before bed. The next thing you know you will be operating from the Sacred Heart and all your actions will express the love you have come to know in your private moments. There will be no tendency to compare yourself, your spiritual experiences, or level of mastery to that of another person. You will begin to feel at one with all that is.

Right now you can choose to tap into the awareness that brings freedom for you to be your authentic and divine self. Gratitude opens your heart and directs your energy toward what you love and what brings you joy. Become aware of the thoughts, feelings, beliefs, attitudes, and choices that are creating your reality. Take responsibility for them and choose those that serve you and your world. Duality *can* exist without conflict. You have free will to do as you please. Your ego will be integrated with the love you have come to bask in. It truly wants the bliss that comes from abiding in the Sacred Heart.

We each have a role to play in bringing about a shift into purer consciousness. We have the power to transmute the law of sin and death into the law of grace. You may be doing this on a soul level without realizing it. If you are transmuting energy for others, be sure to work with your team of spirit guides, ascended masters, angels, archangels, and other pure beings of light to keep your own light burning bright. This will draw people to the healing light and love of the universe, and allow you to be a vessel of healing light, rather than being drained of your personal energy.

Once entering the ascension process, you cannot go back to the limited self you once were. This is a personal and individual journey we must all make, but we are not alone. We have the very presence of the Holy Spirit as well as our ascended forefathers and foremothers, our spirit guides, enlightened beings, and each other to lend support. As Anastasia says, "We will be carried across the illusion of time and darkness and we will take others with us." The choice then is to embrace the change our life's experience is bringing to our soul, and make the most of this amazing opportunity for your own personal evolution.

The Mayan calendar ends in 2012 because the future is ours to create. We are writing our history and our future with every thought we think. Whether is it the end of the world through natural or human disaster, or the New Heaven and New Earth, we are creating what we will experience next. Thus, it's is a great time to be on the planet and help facilitate this shift into purer consciousness.

Fear-based practices and beliefs that do not serve the light are fading away as we align with the Divine Mother's ability to recognize and feel emotion without judgment. What remains then is the loving energy of the Sacred Heart that assures our ascension.

The timeless theme, earth and heaven will pass away. It's not a dream: God will make all things new that day. Gone is the curse from which I stumbled and fell. Evil is banished to eternal hell. No more night. No more pain. No more tears. Never crying again. And praises to the great I AM. We will live in the light of the risen lamb.

~ Walt Harrah, "No More Night"

Now is the time to fully realize what it means to be spiritual beings having a human experience, and know that together we can make the dream of world peace come true. Like a caterpillar, pushing its way out of the cocoon, our true authentic self is about to take flight! We are ushering in a kingdom of light and love in which all are innocent, where peace abides, and cooperation for the good of all is manifested. The illusion of death, dying, and separation are being replaced with the sweetness of eternal oneness in the nurturing love of the Divine Mother. Get excited about the future, own your power, and let's

He that hath an ear, let him hear what the Spirit saith unto the churches: To him that overcometh will I give to eat of the tree of life [immortalilty], which is in the midst of the paradise of God.

~ Revelation 2:7

manifest the New Earth that is about to peek over the horizon!

We are moving back to Paradise—back to the Garden of Eden (oneness with God, having no limited or false beliefs), and we will soon begin to realize the immortality of the human body joined with the spiritual body. Our cup will be overflowing with our divine nature as we spend time in the ecstatic union with God-Goddess. Let's embrace the high vibration of gratitude, love, and joy, which release the essence of our true nature.

I hope this book has helped you learn more about why you are here, and why submitting to the purification process toward having purer thoughts needs to be your focus. I trust you will be able to understand and embrace the planetary and personal changes (even the chaos and temporary discomfort as old issues are cleared) that the shift into purer consciousness is causing.

It is my wish that you allow the Christ consciousness to be birthed in and through you; and that your immortal light body be activated for inner-dimensional travel as the accelerated frequencies of pure love are anchored on Earth.

I pray that you have an increased capacity for compassion and unconditional love as you come into union with your Creator. May you accept, feel, and become one with the energy of love as we merge with the indwelling Christ arising on Earth. Together, let's evolve our thinking, attuning it to the love and light of God-Goddess, so we may outwardly radiate the truth—the oneness we have with Spirit—into our world and create harmony and world peace.

About the Author

Yvonne Perry is a metaphysical teacher, podcast host, and published author of numerous books that help people on a spiritual path. A graduate of American Institute of Holistic Theology, Yvonne holds a Bachelor of Science in Metaphysics.

Ms. Perry offers coaching to help people personally discover the spiritual purpose for which they have been sent to the planet. No matter where you are in managing energy, she can intuitively help you take the next step toward accomplishing your divine mission. Working with the ascended masters, she can help you get clear and start living a fulfilled, joyful, peaceful life that comes from being in alignment with your higher self or oversoul.

Bibliography

"About Do As One." *Do As One*. 15 March 2012 <http://doasone.org/About_2.htm>.

"All of Creation is Moving Light." *Sacred Geometry*. SpiralofLight.com. 8 March 2012 <http://www.spiraloflight.com/ls_sacred.html>.

"Does NLP work? Is it the basis of Derren Brown's 'mind control' act?" *TheStraightDope.com*. 20 November 2007. The Straight Dope Science Advisory Board. 8 March 2012 <http://www.straightdope.com/columns/read/2272/does-nlp-work>.

"Hariakhan Babaji Maharaj." *Cosmicharmony.com*. 14 January 2012 <http://www.cosmicharmony.com/Sp/Babaji/Babaji.htm>.

"Nephilim." *Wikipedia: The Free Encyclopedia*. Wikimedia Foundation, Inc. 15 March 2012 <http://en.wikipedia.org/wiki/Nephilim>.

"NeuroLinguistic Programming." *Holisticonline.com*. 1 January 2004. 8 March 2012 <http://www.holisticonline.com/hol_neurolinguistic.htm>.

"Sacred Geometry." *Wikipedia: The Free Encyclopedia*. Wikimedia Foundation, Inc. 14 January 2012 <http://en.wikipedia.org/wiki/Sacred_geometry>.

"Suspended Animation." *Wikipedia: The Free Encyclopedia*. Wikimedia Foundation, Inc. 5 February 2012 <http://en.wikipedia.org/wiki/Suspended_animation>.

"Tibetan singing bowl." *Wikipedia: The Free Encyclopedia*. Wikimedia Foundation, Inc. 5 February 2012 <http://en.wikipedia.org/wiki/Singing_bowl>.

"What is a Walk-in and What Do They Do?" *GreatDreams.com*. 16 June 2007. 14 January 2012 <http://www.greatdreams.com/walkin.htm>.

"Who is Babaji?" *Babaji.net*. 14 January 2012 <http://www.babaji.net/teachings-babaji.htm>.

Akemi. "Ascension and Enlightenment." *Real Life Spirituality*. 13 July 2009. 12 January 2012 <http://reallifespirituality.com/ascension-and-enlightenment/>.

Akemi. "Ascension Soul Shifts or Walk-Ins." *Real Life Spirituality*. 22 February 2009. 12 January 2012 <http://reallifespirituality.com/ascension-soul-shifts-walk-ins/>.

Akemi. "Demystifying Starseeds, Walk-Ins and Lightworkers." *Real Life Spirituality*. 27 October 2009. 12 January 2012. <http://reallifespirituality.com/starseeds-walk-ins-lightworkers>.

Akemi. "Starseeds: Pleiadians." *Real Life Spirituality.* 21 June 2009. 12 January 2012 <http://reallifespirituality.com/starseeds-pleiadians/>.

Allison, Susan. Empowered Healer. Bloomington, Indiana. Balboa Press, 2011.

Beaconsfield, Hannah. Welcome to Planet Earth: A Guide for Walk-ins and Starseeds. Sedona, AZ: Light Technology Productions, 1997.

Belton, Aine. "10 Ways to Raise Your Consciousness." *Global Love Project.* 21 November 2011. 21 November 2011 <http://globalloveproject.com/2011/11/10-ways/>.

King James Version of the Holy Bible. *BibleGateway.com.* <http://www.biblegateway.com>.

Bhagavan, Amma. Oneness Existing to Living. *Oneness University.* 10 April 2012. <http://www.onenessuniversity.org>.

Braden, Gregg. "Secrets of the Lost Mode of Prayer." *YouTube.* 9 October 2009. 17 February 2012 <http://www.youtube.com/watch?v=Zt6bMz96YPU>.

Braden, Gregg. The Spontaneous Healing of Belief: Shattering the Paradigm of False Limits. Carlsbad, CA: Hay House, 2008.

Chapman, Rev. Kari. "WALK-INS: on earth assignment." *The Namaste Healing Center.* 27 March 2012 <http://www.namaste-wi.com/walk-in.htm>

Chief Standing Elk. *Starknowledge TV.* 29 February 2012 <http://star-knowledge.net/01law_of_free_will.htm>.

Creme, Benjamin. "Transmission: A Meditation for the New Age." *Share International.* <http://www.Share-International.org/transmission>.

Crystal, Ellie. "Merkabah." *Crystalinks.com.* 15 March, 2012 <http://www.crystalinks.com/merkaba.html>.

Danrich, Karen Mila. "The Symptoms of Ascension." 27 April 2000. 28 February 2012 <http://www.selftransform.net/Ascension_Symptoms.htm>.

Fitzpatrick, Owen. "003 How does NLP work." *YouTube.* 13 July 2009. 8 March 2012. <http://www.youtube.com/watch?v=C1txO6gP_f4>.

FreeYogaVideos. "Yoga Breathing for Beginners." *YouTube.* 12 April 2009. 5 March 2012 <http://www.youtube.com/watch?v=VS-9fXmUt-c>.

Freeyourmind4evr. "Extraterrestrials." *YouTube.* 21 October 2009. 8 March 2012 <http://youtu.be/ClvUqyeTcoQ>.

Freeyourmind4evr. "Multidimensional: Merkaba." *YouTube.* 12 September 2009. 14 January 2012 <http://www.youtube.com/watch?v=21tZI3Hc12E>.

Giorgio, Dr. Laura De. "Brainwave Synchronization." *DeepTranceNow.com*. 8 March 2012 <http://www.deeptrancenow.com/brainwave_synchronization.htm>.

Giorgio, Dr. Laura De. "Subliminal Messages Research." *DeepTranceNow.com*. 8 March 2012 <http://www.deeptrancenow.com/subliminal_messages.htm>.

Goode, Tom, Ph.D. "Full Wave Breathing Exercises." *YouTube*. 27 July 2009. 15 March 2012 <http://youtu.be/9frOB16m-yw>.

Goode, Tom, Ph.D. Breathe and Grow Rich. N.p.: SmashWords.com, May 2010.

Hand, Barbara Clow. Catastrophobia: The Truth Behind Earth Changes in the Coming Age of Light. Rochester, VA: Bear & Company, 2001.

Harrah, Walt. "No More Night." Word Music, 1983.

Harris, Tom. "How Hypnosis Works." *HowStuffWorks.com*. 15 March 2012 <http://science.howstuffworks.com/science-vs-myth/extrasensory-perceptions/hypnosis1.htm>.

Haughton, Brian. "Suspended Animation." *MysteriousPeople.com*. 2003. 5 February 2012 <http://www.mysteriouspeople.com/suspended_animation.htm>.

Heartsong, Claire. Anna, Grandmother of Jesus. Santa Clara, CA: Spiritual Endeavors Education Publishing Co., 2002.

Kardec, Allan. The Spirit's Book. Las Vegas, NV: Brotherhood of Life Books, 1989.

Kelemeria Myarea Elohim. "Interview with a Walk-In." *The Salem New Age Center*. 10 April 2012. <http://www.salemctr.com/newage/center14.html>.

King, Godfré Ray. Unveiled Mysteries. Pg. 64. Chicago, IL: Saint Germain Press, 1939.

Lawrience, David. "Top 10 Tips Indicating Signs of Spiritual Awakening/Enlightenment." *Emotional Health & Energy Healing Tips*. 17 October 2011. 12 January 2012 <http://www.emotionalhealthtips.com/10-tips-spiritual-awakening-6>.

Marciniak, Barbara. Path of Empowerment. Novato, CA: New World Library, 2004.

Megre, Vladimir. Anastasia (The Ringing Cedars, Book 1). Kahului, HI: Ringing Cedars Press, 1996.

Megré, Vladimir. The Ringing Cedars of Russia (The Ringing Cedars, Book 2). Kahului, HI: Ringing Cedars Press, 1996.

Mitchell, Karyn K. Walk-Ins Soul Exchange. St. Charles, IL: Mind Rivers Publications, 1999.

Parrish-Harra, Rev. E. Carol, Ph.D. <u>Love is a Promise, a Discipline, and a Lifestyle</u>. Self-published E-book, 2011.

Pittman, Ross. "7-Step Prayer Success Formula." *Conscious Life News*. 7 March 2011. 17 February 2012 <http://consciouslifenews.com/7-step-prayer-success-formula/115391/>.

Pixie, Magenta. "Dis Ease Illness and Ascension Syndrome." *YouTube*. 11 November 2011 <http://www.youtube.com/watch?v=ihV6SPXH15w>.

Ray, Sondra and Mark Sullivan. "What is Liberation Breathing®." *LiberationBreathing.com*. 15 March 2012 <https://www.liberationbreathing.com>.

Ray, Sondra. <u>How to Be Chic, Fabulous, and Live Forever</u>. Berkeley, CA: Celestial Arts, 1995.

Rich, Simona. "Kundalini Energy." *Personal Development Coach*. 12 January 2012 <http://www.personal-development-coach.net/kundalini-energy.html>.

Shier, Susann Taylor. <u>Soul Reunion: The Return Home from Separation</u>. Boulder, CO: Velvet Spring Press, 2011.

Shumsky, Susan. <u>Ascension, Connecting with the Immortal Masters and Beings of Light</u>. Franklin Lakes, NJ: New Page Books, 2010.

Skarin, Annalee. <u>Beyond Mortal Boundaries</u>. Los Angeles, CA: DeVorss, 1969.

Starr, Jelaila. "Solutions for Ascension Symptoms." *SelfGrowth.com*. 24 January 2012 <http://www.selfgrowth.com/articles/solutions_for_ascension_symptoms>.

Tachi-ren, Tashira channeling Archangel Ariel. <u>What is Lightbody?</u> Lithia Springs, GA: WorldTree Press, 2007.

TheSpiritScience. "Spirit Science 1 - Thoughts (Revised)." *YouTube*. 20 January 2012. 8 March 2012. <http://www.youtube.com/watch?v=xmN2RL4VJsE>.

Treasure, Julian. "Julian Treasure: The 4 Ways Sound Affects Us." *TED*. October 2009. 15 March 2012 <http://www.ted.com/talks/julian_treasure_the_4_ways_sound_affects_us.html>.

Tuttle, Dr. Will. <u>The World Peace Diet</u>. New York, NY: Lantern Books, 2005.

Virtue, Doreen. <u>Earth Angels: A Pocket Guide for Incarnated Angels, Elementals, Starpeople, Walk-ins, and Wizards</u>. Carlsbad, CA: Hay House, 2002.

Vorly, Ethan. "Learn the Truth about Tantric Sex." *Tantric Secrets*. 15 March 2012 <http://www.tantricsecrets.com>.

Vorly, Ethan. "What are Entities?" *EntityClearing.com*. 12 January 2012
    <http://www.entityclearing.com/clearing.htm>.

"Walk-Ins." *CrystalLinks.com*. 12 January 2012
    <http://www.crystalinks.com/walk_ins.html>.

Warri9. "10 Signs of a Spiritual Awakening." <u>YouTube</u>. 29 August 2010. 11 January
    2012 <http://www.youtube.com/watch?v=txTsbeuY5gM>.

Resources

Learn more about awakening at http://www.onenessuniversity.org

Take this quiz to see if you are a walk-in soul.
http://healing.about.com/library/quiz/walk-in/bl-walk-in-quiz.htm

Tell your walk-in story online at
http://healing.about.com/b/2009/03/05/walk-in-theories-and-soul-possession.htm

Information about Pleiadian walk-ins
http://lightworkers.org/wisdom/89851/pleiadian-agenda.

Walk-in Evolution International
http://walkinevolution.blogspot.com/

Empath Connection on Facebook:
http://www.facebook.com/pages/Empath-Connection/134926033194344

Videos about Spiritists' views: http://www.spiritistvideos.com.

WeAreOneinSpirit Youtube channel.
http://www.youtube.com/user/WeAreOneinSpirit/featured.

Get a free audio book, *Bliss in Divine Oneness*, based on teachings from *A Course in Miracles* at
http://weareoneinspirit.blogspot.com/p/join.html.

Great thoughts on physical immortality:
http://physicalimmortalitythemasspossibility.wordpress.com.

The World Peace Diet by Dr. Will Tuttle is a must for anyone on the fence about the vegan lifestyle. See
http://www.worldpeacediet.org to download the e-book and CD.

Download "Living in Harmony with All Life" - an audio discourse by Dr. Will Tuttle at http://www.worldpeacediet.org/download.htm

Find a practitioner in your area via the American Association of Naturopathic Physicians http://www.naturopathic.org/

ENERGIES
20- New Ones
23- Matrix

SouL
(20) EXPansion

EARTH
22 - 23 Speed
Conc. = Vibes

Conc | 23 | 25

Lower
VIBES = Darkness (25)
26